Delight for a wretched man

DELIGHT FOR A WRETCHED MAN

Romans 7 and the doctrine of sanctification

A. Benjamin R. Clark

 EVANGELICAL PRESS

EVANGELICAL PRESS
12 Wooler Street, Darlington, Co. Durham, DL1 1RQ, England

© Evangelical Press 1993
First Published 1993

British Library Cataloguing in Publication Data available

ISBN 0-85234-311-6

Printed and bound in Great Britain at the Bath Press, Avon

To Geraldine, Nicola and Martyn,
'heirs together of the grace of life' (1 Peter 3:7),
who delight in the things of God,
are constant in faith,
and precious ministers of encouragement (Eph. 5:29).

Contents

Preface

This book has been written in the earnest desire that it might make some small contribution to an understanding of the doctrine of sanctification in general, and Romans chapter 7 in particular. James Denney once said, 'To be saved from sin, a man must at the same time own it and disown it.' It is my conviction that Paul does just that in the chapter we are considering. Only a regenerate man can describe the unbelieving state as the apostle does here; and only a man who takes his own sin seriously will cry out as does the apostle.

As we follow the unfolding theme of these verses, my prayer is that the Holy Spirit will not only give us to understand the importance of the principles relating to sanctification which are enumerated in our conclusion, but that we might be sanctified by the Spirit through the truth of God's Word.

The subject under discussion is a controversial one. It is a sad fact of history that disagreements over this chapter in Romans, and over sanctification, have too often been expressed in an uncharitable and hostile spirit so that, rather than furthering the experience of sanctification, they have resulted in the grieving of the Spirit. I trust that those whose understanding differs from the one expressed in these pages will not feel that the author despises or belittles them. Many with whose views I disagree have been giants of the faith, in comparison with whom the present writer is a spiritual pygmy. Yet I believe that in love I may dare to express a contrary view without denigrating a brother in the Lord.

In this study we shall attempt to follow the unfolding argumentation of Paul as he moves logically and carefully towards the implications of the gospel for a life of holiness. The scriptural passages are not easy, as the multiplicity of divergent views indicates. Nevertheless, if we accept the doctrine of the perspicuity of Scripture we can be confident that, through a careful and prayerful study of the text, the Holy Spirit will grant us understanding. While a detailed study of Romans 7 will never be light reading, my prayer is that as the attentive reader accompanies me on a journey of exploration through these pages of God's Word, he or she will be thrilled as we consider together the great truths proclaimed in this remarkable epistle.

It is my hope that the closely reasoned argumentation of the early part of the book will not detract from the important principles enunciated in the closing chapter. Conversely, I hope that those principles will be seen to be firmly rooted in Scripture, and that the cry of the so-called 'wretched man' of Romans 7 will be ours, and that we too will rejoice in the assurance that victory will be ours 'through Jesus Christ our Lord'.

A. Benjamin R. Clark

1.
Setting the scene

Throughout the history of the Christian church the doctrine of sanctification has been surrounded by great controversy. This is hardly surprising, since it is precisely in this area that conflicting theological systems find practical expression. Sanctification is for this reason a subject of the utmost importance. The whole purpose of biblical revelation is to produce men and women of God. Holiness is no optional extra for the Christian.

We live in an age when the vocabulary of sanctification has virtually dropped out of evangelical language. We rarely refer to individuals as 'godly', 'saintly', or 'holy'. This is more than just a matter of vocabulary. The concept of personal godliness seems no longer to be a subject of primary concern. The theological confusion which prevails today has caused many to speak of their experiences, their gifts, or their activities, rather than of their God and their longing to be conformed to his likeness. We need to recover the biblical doctrine of sanctification.

Romans 7 is one of the most memorable passages in the writings of Paul. It expresses vividly man's moral struggle with imperfection and contains the heart-rending cry: 'Who shall deliver me out of the body of this death?' (literal translation). But what are we to make of this cry? Who utters it? And what is he yearning for? The answers we give to these questions will inevitably have a strong bearing on our understanding of the doctrine of sanctification. Who is this 'miserable sinner' who expresses himself so plaintively? Is it Paul himself, or is he merely using a literary device? If it is Paul, is he speaking of himself as a Christian, or is he referring back to his unregenerate days, when his experience was one of futility and spiritual bankruptcy? If it is the language of a true child of God, is such an expression of defeat and frustration compatible with the tone of victory of chapter 8? Might it not rather be the description of a carnal or immature Christian, an 'unsanctified Christian', who has experienced only the new birth, but who knows nothing of victory and release from struggle through the Holy Spirit? Or can it possibly be the description of a permanent and significant element in Paul's mature Christian life?

These are very important questions. Our understanding of the doctrine of sanctification must not only be able to accommodate what Paul says in Romans 7; it must be entirely consistent with it, and must take very seriously the great truths Paul brings before us in these remarkable chapters of Holy Scripture.

Historically there has been no agreement among theologians concerning the meaning of Romans 7. Rival systems of theology have adopted conflicting views of this passage. We are able to identify four distinct points of view which have been expressed by Christian leaders over the years.

1. 'Miserable because unbelieving'

This view, which has widespread acceptance, holds that the person alluded to in Romans 7, whether Paul himself or someone else, is unregenerate, and what is described is pre-Christian experience.

This view largely predominated during the first three centuries of the Christian church, and was championed by many of the early Greek fathers, including Origen and Tertullian. Grotius is so delighted in discovering this fact that he exclaims in ecstasy, 'Praise be to God that the best Christians, those of the first three centuries, understood this place as they ought!' Augustine, too, in the early part of his life, held that this passage must be applied to pre-Christian experience.

While many of the Reformers rejected this understanding of the passage, preferring to see it as describing true Christian experience, Humanists, such as Erasmus and Faber, continued to expound it as depicting the misery of the unconverted sinner. But they did so with a subtle but significant variation. They rejected the Reformed doctrine of the total depravity of man's nature, and viewed Romans

7 in terms of dualism within man himself. He was a split personality, torn between a desire to do both good and evil. However, they continued to see the passage as speaking of man outside of Christ, man in sin.

It was Pietism which rejected most energetically the teaching of the Protestant Reformers that the passage described authentic Christian experience. Pietism began among Protestants in the seventeenth and eighteenth centuries in Germany, at a time when the churches had become entangled in confessional rigidity. It was what became known as 'the Age of Orthodoxy', or the period of 'Protestant Scholasticism'. The ideas of the Reformers seemed to have become so systematized and schematized in confessions and creeds that it appeared that the truth had been fossilized. Little attention was being paid to the necessity of good works and personal godliness. Against this cold orthodoxy Pietists such as Spener and Franck reacted, and as part of their reaction they condemned the sins of their day. Spener issued a call for reformation, including an appeal for a better knowledge of the Bible itself on the part of the people, the restoration of mutual Christian concern, an emphasis on good works and a restoration of preaching to make it more fervent.

Historians disagree as to the nature of Pietism. Some feel it was essentially a revival of medieval and monastic piety stimulated by contact with the Puritans. Others believe it represented progress in Lutheranism, and development towards biblical Christianity. Whatever view one takes of this movement, Pietism undoubtedly fostered a desire for holy living, biblical scholarship and missions.

It was their concern for holy living which caused Pietists to declare that Paul's statements in Romans 7:14-25 could only refer to the unconverted, unregenerate man. Because of dogmatic considerations, notably their view of the meaning of sanctification and the Christian life, they considered it was utterly inconceivable that Paul should speak as he does if he had in mind his new life as a Christian. The internal discord described in the passage ruled his life while he was under the law, knowing nothing of grace and life in the Spirit. The prolonged and desolating nightmare which issues in the agonized cry for deliverance was seen to reflect human experience outside of Christ.

Over the centuries this view of the passage continued to be heard, and increasingly came to predominate over rival theories. The balance of opinion over recent years has favoured this approach, though often with slight variations and modifications. Notable expositors have insisted that the Paul of Romans 7:14-25 is the same as the one of 7:7-13, but a different Paul from the exuberant and triumphant one of Romans 8. Thus J. Weiss writes, 'What would be the use of the new birth or redemption if it did not end the miserable stress and slavery?' A. E. Garvie agrees: 'To apply all that precedes this verse [7:25] to Paul as a Christian would be to admit practically that the grace of God is as powerless against sin as the law is.' J. S. Stewart similarly declares, 'What we read in Romans 7 is the experience of a life requiring to be born again.' C. H. Dodd concludes that the passage is to be understood as 'an authentic transcript of Paul's own experience during the period which culminated in his vision on the road to Damascus'.[1]

Variations of the unregenerate view

A variation of this view holds that the passage represents Paul's assessment *through Christian eyes* of his former unregenerate state. Most modern monographs on this chapter show considerable agreement with Kümmel, who argues strongly for this understanding of the passage. He maintains that the real theme in Romans 7 is the significance of the law, not simply the subjective experience of salvation.[2]

Here again we notice another variation of the traditional Greek view. Romans 7 is viewed by Kümmel as dealing with the significance of Christ and the Holy Spirit in the context of *salvation history,* rather than in the context of personal experience and ethics. Althaus thus maintains that in this chapter Paul describes the history of every man in Adam.[3]

The view of Ridderbos also fits into this broad view that the passage applies to the unregenerate man. According to him, Romans 7 and 8 are concerned with redemptive-historical contrasts, not with individual experiences. The real subject is the antithesis between law and Spirit, the impotence of mankind outside of Christ and the power of the Spirit to break through the barrier of sin and the flesh to any degree at all. He understands the personal setting of the passage as the representation of the moral man shackled by the law, with whom Paul identifies himself, and of whom he writes from the viewpoint of one who now has faith.[4]

Bultmann is so confident that this is the correct interpretation of the passage that he contemptuously sweeps aside any dissident voice: 'It seems to me that sufficient discussion has been given to this problem. There can no longer be any doubt as to the answer. It is fundamentally the status of man under the law which is characterized here, and it is seen through the eyes of one whom Christ has freed from law.'[5] Käseman makes a similar sweeping generalization: 'Paul is depicting pre-Christian being from a Christian standpoint (as is generally agreed since Kümmel's monograph).'[6]

Finally we note the views of Dr Martyn Lloyd-Jones. In his published sermons he rejects forcefully the idea that the passage refers to unregenerate man.[7] Nevertheless, despite his protestations, the view he propounds has much in common with the one he rejects. According to him, the man in Romans 7 is an unconverted man, but one who is *experiencing conviction of sin,* as the Holy Spirit reveals to him the depravity of his heart.

Dr Lloyd-Jones holds that in this section of Romans 7, 'The theme is the law, what it does do, what it does not do, what it cannot do. The Apostle is not primarily writing about himself or his own experience, but about the law and the truth about the law.' The whole of chapter 7 is viewed as relating to one great theme, the function and limits of the law. Paul is thought to be answering charges brought against him with respect to his teaching concerning the law — that he was dismissing the law altogether, that the law is sin, that the ministry of the law was a ministry of death. The confessions and agonies of the final section relate, according to Lloyd-Jones, not to a believer nor an unbeliever, but to a mind illuminated by the Holy Spirit to see the holiness of the law and the sinfulness of his own heart. It describes a man who is experiencing intense conviction of sin, who feels utterly condemned. 'He is aware of his weakness for the first time, and his complete failure. But he does not know any more. He is trying to keep the law in his own strength, and he finds that he cannot. He therefore feels condemned; he is under conviction. He does not know, he does not understand the truth of the gospel, about salvation in and through Jesus Christ.'[8]

Thus according to Dr Lloyd-Jones, the man of Romans 7 is still the unregenerate man, though under conviction of sin. His position is a minor qualification of the non-Reformed tradition of exegesis of this chapter. He too refuses to accept that Romans 7 could describe mature Christian experience in the full sense of the term.

Common to all these writers is the conviction that Romans 7:14-25 does not represent the experience of a believer, as he longs after holiness. They all hold that the person in question is unregenerate. They may differ and disagree about details of exegesis — whether or not it is Paul himself or someone else, or humanity in general, or a convicted unbeliever — but they all argue strongly that the passage is descriptive of the state and condition of the unbelieving heart, and that it does not represent normative Christian experience. Thus we may describe this as the 'unregenerate view'.

2. Normative Christian experience

A second view, which for identification purposes we shall refer to as the 'Reformed view', since it was the position largely adopted by the Protestant Reformers of the sixteenth century, sees the passage as describing the experience of a regenerate man and as reflecting normative Christian experience.

Once again there is evidence that there were those of the early fathers who, despite the prevalence of the Greek view, held that the passage must be applied to the experience of believers. Augustine adopted this position in the latter part of his life, but acknowledged that he was not the first to suggest it. He says, 'Hence it came to pass that I came to understand these things, as Hilary, Gregory and other holy and famous doctors of the church understood them, who thought that the apostle himself strenuously struggled against carnal lusts, which he was unwilling to have, and yet had, and that he bore witness to the conflict in these words.'[9]

Augustine's interpretation of Romans 7 is interesting for two reasons: firstly, because his views altered and evolved over the years; and secondly, because of his influence on subsequent opinion. His early opinion was that the last section of Romans 7 could not possibly apply to someone in a state of grace. Subsequently, however, he was to alter his view radically. As his Christian experience deepened, giving him deeper insight into his own heart, and as his understanding of Scripture increased, possibly as a direct result of his conflict with Pelagius, he came to regard

Romans 7 as autobiography. He saw verses 14-25 as depicting Paul's present experience — Paul the believer, that is, wrestling with covetousness, and now by God's grace conscious of sin within his own regenerate heart. Divine grace, he insisted, gives not only salvation, but an ever-deepening consciousness and knowledge of sin.

Augustine's mature view was largely accepted by the churches of the Middle Ages, and by the Reformers, including Luther, Calvin, Melanchthon and Beza.

Luther saw in Romans 7 an echo of his own dramatic personal experience, both of conversion and of continuing conflict with remaining sin. Paul, after his conversion, remained a sinner, though a regenerate sinner, like every other Christian. According to Luther, Romans 7 contains the portrait of Paul's post-conversion experience, and depicts the agony of a regenerate man whose heart is torn because of remaining sin within his members.

Calvin, too, insisted on the Christian's experience of liberation, through conversion, from the yoke of slavery to sin. Yet he applied Romans 7 to the Christian: 'Paul proposes the example of a regenerate man, and in this case the law of the Lord so contends with the remains of the flesh, that the spirit yields it obedience... You here therefore see the divided state of believers, from which the contest between the spirit and flesh arises, elegantly termed by Augustine "the Christian warfare and combat".'[10] Calvin sees in the passage the combat of faith which is made necessary throughout the earthly existence of a believer because the relics of sin, while no longer dominating him, yet remain in him.

The great Reformed confessions of faith hold to the same doctrine of sanctification as the Protestant Reformers, and speak of spiritual conflict within the life of a believer, as grace counteracts sin. The *Confession of La Rochelle,* the *Belgic Confession,* the *Heidelberg Catechism* and the *Westminster Confession of Faith,* when presenting the doctrine of sanctification, all quote Romans 7 among proof-texts, thereby showing that the compilers and adherents of these confessions viewed the chapter as depicting the Christian experience of conflict as a result of remaining sin.

This Reformed view was presented vigorously by Puritan writers such as Owen, Charnock and Goodwin, and endorsed by a long line of expositors who, while differing occasionally on details, have maintained that Paul in Romans 7 is referring to himself as a believer, and to believers in general. These include H. Bavinck, L. Berkhof, G. Berkouwer, F. F. Bruce, C. E. B. Cranfield, J. Fraser, R. Haldane, C. Hodge, A. Kuyper, R. C. Lenski, J. Murray and A. Nygren.

3. An unsanctified Christian

A third view is that of Perfectionism and higher-life theories of sanctification. Here Romans 7 is understood as depicting the experience of a carnal believer. He is deemed to be a Christian whose experience falls far short of what it should be. Despite his regeneration, he knows only heartbreaking defeat and frustration, and consequently longs for deliverance.

The influence of John Wesley

This view began to emerge as a result of the ministry of John Wesley in the eighteenth century. While he himself adhered to the Greek or unregenerate view of Romans 7, he was to be one of the formative influences of subsequent higher-life theories of sanctification, and the father of all modern holiness movements. With regard to Romans 7, he felt a deep affinity with the apostle Paul because of his own experiences of sin and salvation. His own conversion to Christ at the age of thirty-four, after long years of strained endeavour and persistent failure, and the victory that came into his life when the power of the Holy Spirit burst in upon him, caused him to feel at one with Paul who had a similar experience. As C. L. Mitton aptly puts it, 'He found in Romans 7 the words which described with uncanny precision his own pre-conversion anguish of heart, and in Romans 8 the very phrases he needed to express the relief and gladness and confidence into which he had been brought.'[11] Wesley expresses himself thus: 'The character assumed [by Paul] is that of a man under the law, and sincerely but ineffectively striving to serve God. To have spoken this of himself or any true believer would have been foreign to the scope of his discourse; nay, utterly contrary to it, and to what is expressly asserted in chapter 8 verse 2, "The law of the Spirit of life has set me free..."'[12]

The importance of Wesley lies not in any novel exegesis of Romans 7 on his part, but in the fact that he taught a doctrine of sanctification, or 'Perfectionism', which encouraged his disciples to propound a new interpretation of the chapter.

We have seen how up to this point lively debate had surrounded the exposition of Romans 7, and how opinions differed as to whether it describes a regenerate or an unregenerate man. Now a third theory began to be propounded, namely that the experience described here is that of an immature, carnal, unsanctified believer, and that this is therefore the expression of abnormal Christianity.

John Wesley himself never claimed perfection, but through his teaching Perfectionism was first given standing within the Protestant church. To support his position he distinguished sharply between justification and sanctification, alleging that they were obtained through separate acts of faith. This meant that there are two types of Christians — those who are only justified, and those who are also sanctified. Exegetically this can be shown to be manifestly wrong.

Some of Wesley's disciples went much further than their master and propounded a less guarded doctrine of Christian Perfectionism. Reacting against the Reformed view, as held by Lutheran Christianity, which seemed to them to console the pious for their sins, and to confirm them in a position of continued imperfection, they viewed Romans 7 as descriptive of an indispensable stage in the Christian life, a state of slavery to sin, of futility and frustration, from which a person is delivered by an experience of 'entire sanctification'. This, according to William Bramwell, for example, is a definitive deliverance from all slavery and condemnation, which a believer can experience some years subsequent to conversion.

Bramwell describes how after his conversion he continued to experience defeat and slavery to sin, just as he had done before he was converted, and precisely as the apostle Paul describes it in Romans 7:22-23. He felt deeply 'the need to be purified from all sin, from every inclination and tendency to sin. It was necessary that the Lord should remove from his heart the principle of sin referred to as the old man, the flesh, the old nature. This he soon experienced; after seeking it by faith he obtained it. He had received the gift of a pure heart.'[13]

Many 'higher-life' movements thus sprang from Wesley, and O. A. Curtis does not exaggerate when he declares, 'Historically, Wesley had almost the same epochal relation to the doctrinal emphasis upon holiness that Luther had to the doctrinal emphasis upon justification by faith, or that Athanasius had on the doctrinal emphasis upon the deity of our Lord.'[14]

We shall have to return to an assessment of these movements later, when we examine the implications of Romans 7 for the doctrine of sanctification. For the moment let it suffice to say that while Wesley himself held to the traditional unregenerate view of Romans 7, his followers viewed the passage as referring to a state of spiritual immaturity from which a person needed to be delivered by moving on into the experience of victory described in chapter 8. All Pietists (and this includes all Perfectionists and all the holiness movements that abound today) who elevate personal sanctification above justification cannot admit that a man like Paul, in a state of grace, still battles against the flesh.

Modified higher-life views

We include here a group of commentators who present a greatly modified form of higher-life teaching, but whose exegesis falls largely within this category.

There are interpreters who take the position that here Paul is not giving a description of a normal or actual Christian life, but of what follows for any man, whether regenerate or unregenerate, who relies upon the law and his own efforts for sanctification. W. H. Griffith Thomas, for example, states, 'The one point of the passage is that it describes a man who is trying to be good and holy by his own efforts and is beaten back every time by the power of indwelling sin. This is the experience of any man who tries this experiment, whether he be regenerate or unregenerate. The experiences here described are certainly not those of the Christian life as it ought to be, and as it may be, the normal Christianity, that is, of chapter 6:17,18; 7:4,6; 8:12; 1 Peter 1:8,9.'[15]

Another example is C. L. Mitton, who sees the passage as describing the distressing experience of a morally earnest man, Christian or not, who attempts to live up to the commands of God on his own, without that constant reliance upon the uninterrupted supply of the resources of God which is the characteristic of the mature Christian.[16]

In a similar manner, D. Wenham and R. K. Y. Fung view the passage as descriptive of the experience of the Christian who attempts to fulfil the law without the full aid of the Spirit.

All the commentators of this general section share a common approach to Romans 7 in that they view it as applying either exclusively or largely to believers, and reject the unregenerate view.

4. The modern liberal approach

Finally, we note briefly a fourth view which is radically different from those we have already outlined. It is that of the radical scholar Karl Barth.

It is difficult to consider the view of Barth according to traditional categories of regeneration or sanctification. He is not so concerned with categories of personal experience as with supra-personal *Heilgeschichte* (history of salvation). He is a dialectic philosopher more than a Christian theologian. For him Romans 7 does not deal with the question of man's experience of God. He places the question outside the arena of history as we know it, and treats religious questions within the area of existential philosophy. Thus it is illegitimate to ask whether in Romans 7 Paul is speaking of man before his conversion or after his conversion. The question relates to a higher existentialist plane. The passage refers to man as man, whether he be religious but outside of Christ, or Christian and united to Christ. There is a philosophical dualism in man, and that is what Paul is describing. Man is by nature a man in contradiction, altogether sinner and altogether sanctified.

It is a mistake to consider Barth as a biblical theologian. He was a speculative philosopher rather than a biblical theologian, and his monistic, universalistic, philosophical presuppositions do not help us in our attempt to understand the significance of the doctrine of sanctification as reflected in Romans 7.

Conclusion

What of the other three options which we have identified in the history of the interpretation of this passage? It is interesting to note that historically the three opinions correspond largely, though not exclusively, with major movements of church history: *the Roman Catholic period* of dominance, when the passage was applied generally to unregenerate man; *the Reformation period,* when it was viewed as descriptive of Christian warfare, and, finally, *the pietist-evangelical movement* of the eighteenth and nineteenth centuries, which applied the passage to the experience of the unspiritual, unsanctified believer in his longing after holiness.

These views were not limited to these specific periods of history, but to a large extent they epitomized the understanding of major historical movements which predominated at different times. Today all three views are to be found in some form or other in contemporary writings, on occasions with devastating consequences for the doctrine of sanctification.

It is my conviction that the second view outlined above, that which we have referred to as the Reformed or regenerate view, alone accords with all that Paul says, both in these specific verses 14 to 25, and in the general context in which the passage is found.

In the chapters which follow I shall attempt to show this to be the correct way of understanding these remarkable verses by considering chapter 7 in its setting in Romans, and by going on to examine the text itself. We shall then be in a position to highlight some important aspects of the biblical doctrine of sanctification.

2.
The triumph of grace in Romans

Romans 7 can only be understood if we see it in relation to the rest of the epistle in general, and chapters 6 to 8, its immediate setting, in particular. It is not an isolated section, unconnected with the rest of the letter, but depends on what has been written up to this point, and in turn provides the platform for what Paul goes on to say in subsequent chapters. Of all the New Testament epistles, none is so clearly structured as Romans. There is a clear overriding theme, a carefully constructed argument and a logical progression towards a practical application of the truths considered. It is always a wise principle of interpretation to consider specific texts in their contexts, but never more so than when we are dealing with carefully developed argumentation, as in the epistle to the Romans.

The centrality of justification by faith

The great theme of Romans is justification by faith. This is the one great comprehensive truth that Paul wants to proclaim. There is a righteousness available for sinners which is not of any human fabrication, a divine righteousness, a righteousness from God, by which sinners are acquitted before the divine judgement seat, a righteousness imputed, received by faith alone. This is the heart of the Christian gospel, a glorious doctrine which distinguishes Christianity from every other religion, and biblical Christianity from all hybrid liberal-rationalistic theologies. The whole of the Christian life depends on this basic Christian truth. And this truth is central to Romans.

In the first chapter Paul declares this stated theme (vv. 16,17): 'He who through faith is righteous shall live.' This is the gospel he is determined to preach at Rome, and this is the gospel he delineates in the chapters which follow.

In the main body of the letter there are three principal sections. Each of these, however, is vitally related to the central theme of justification by faith.

Romans 1-8. Righteousness is required by God, and is obtainable by faith alone, for Jew and Gentile alike.

Romans 9 to 11. The rejection of Israel is not incompatible with justification by faith. Israel had failed to understand God's grace in offering free justification on the basis of Christ's imputed righteousness. Did this mean that God had abrogated his promise to Israel? If this were so, could God not be charged with unfaithfulness to his own word?

In these three chapters Paul resolves this charge in the doctrine of God's sovereignty. The promises of God to Israel are not abrogated by the gospel of grace (9:1-5). The promise is only to those who believe (9:6-29). Israel is herself responsible for her rejection because she seeks her righteousness through the law (9:30 - 10:21). When her time comes, Israel will be accepted by God's free compassion (ch. 11).

Romans 12 to 15. Righteousness must be manifested in moral conduct. Those who by faith are righteous must live according to righteousness. This was the emphasis of Habakkuk's declaration, and Paul does not hesitate to declare that faith works. 'By faith the just *shall live*' (Hab. 2:4). To be justified by faith does not undermine morality. Rather it secures it. There is no antinomianism in the thought of Paul; nor had there been in chapter 6. But Paul deals here with concrete and practical duties devolving upon believers. These particularly concern their relations to one another within the Christian community. But since believers sustain relations with other men and institutions, Paul deals with Christian behaviour in the exercise of their social and political responsibilities.

These three distinguishable sections do not deal with separate themes, and must not mask the unbroken unity of the letter as a whole. Paul's concern is to proclaim justification by faith alone. He answers objections which might arise as a result of the rejection by the Jews of God's grace in Christ. He deals with the question of the Jews simply because of the burning issue of Israel's rejection, and the possibility that this could lead to allegations that God was unfaithful to his promises concerning his ancient people. God's acquittal of sinners on the basis of faith in Christ and his redemptive work, as described in the first eight chapters, resulted in God's cutting off of Israel. But this seemed to impinge on the very nature of God and the reliability of his promises concerning the salvation of Israel. Paul proceeds, then, to show that justification by faith, rather than undermining the whole Old Testament revelation of God's plan for Israel, in fact establishes it.

Similarly chapters 12-15 do not deal with a separate issue, but demonstrate how Christian ethics presuppose, and derive from, the grace of God revealed in the gospel. 'I beseech you *therefore* [that is, on the basis of all I have been saying hitherto] by *the mercies of God* [which in effect have been the substance of my epistle] to present your bodies in a living sacrifice... Do not be conformed to this world, but be transformed by the renewing of your mind' (12:1-2, NKJV). He then proceeds to give practical illustrations of the application of this exhortation in the subsequent chapters.

The implications of justification by faith (Romans 5-8)

In the first four chapters Paul vigorously presents the doctrine of justification by faith. He does so with juridical precision, arguing first negatively, to establish the need for divine grace, then positively, to show the appropriateness of Christ's atoning work.

He establishes: firstly, the need for justification; secondly, its equal terms for Jew and Gentile; and thirdly, that the one appointed condition for salvation is faith in Christ's atoning work (3:25), that is, personal trustful acceptance of Christ's work of propitiation and expiation. Fourthly, he illustrates the nature and response of faith by referring to Abraham, so proving that Jew and Gentile alike are justified on the same basis and conditions.

Up to this point Paul has concentrated on one application of Habakkuk's statement: 'It is *by faith* that the just have life.' He has shown that eternal life is offered to sinners on the condition of faith in Christ's redeeming work. Starting with chapter 5 he makes a new application of the same text. His task during the next four chapters is to show what it means to say that 'He who through faith is righteous *shall live.*' He concentrates on demonstrating in general terms what it means to have life in Christ. He will delay until chapter 12 his exposition of the practical outworkings of this in terms of day-to-day living. But in chapters 5 to 8 he defines that life which is received by faith in Christ in its relationship to the great powers which confined us in a situation of death until Christ set us free.[1]

How important it is for us to realize the vital connection which exists between Christian doctrine and Christian living! Justification by faith is not merely the central doctrine of our faith; it is what guarantees for the believer both a standing before God and a life free from the dominion of the tyrants to which hitherto he has been in bondage. In a word, through the power of the Holy Spirit he has been set free to live unto God.

This is Paul's great theme in chapters 5 to 8. Step by step he will depict, sometimes with deep intensity of feeling, the glorious emancipating power of the gospel over the destructive powers which once held us in their thraldom, wrath, sin, law and death.

Something radically new — two contrasting ages

But first of all in chapter 5 the apostle establishes the contrast between life in the old age of tyranny and sin with life in the new age of liberty and forgiveness. In the first eleven verses he does so in a triumphant paeon of praise in which he rejoices in the consequences of justification. He declares that, having been justified through faith in Christ, we have peace with God; we have access to grace in which we stand; we rejoice, despite all our sufferings. Further, to us has been bequeathed the Holy Spirit. All these blessings have come to us through Christ, who died for sinners. Then from verse 12 onwards, in the parallel he draws between Adam and Christ, Paul contrasts the age of death, which ensued upon Adam's transgression, with the age of life which Christ has established. The old age of sin, judgement and death in Adam is contrasted with the age of grace, righteousness and justification in Christ.

Paul concluded the first part of his epistle by coupling the two ideas of justification and resurrection. Christ 'was raised ... for our justification' (4:25). He now proceeds to link the two ideas with reference to the experience of the believer. Just as the resurrection of Christ assures the justification of the sinner, so the justification of the sinner assures his resurrection to newness of life. Christ's resurrection inaugurates the new age of life. In this way, the Christian life is set in the framework of the new age of life inaugurated by Christ's resurrection. To be justified is 'to pass from death to life' (John 5:24). God has 'delivered us from the power of darkness and ... translated us into the kingdom of the Son of his love' (Col. 1:13, NKJV). The mention of the kingdom points to the cosmic and eschatological fulfilment in heaven itself.

In Romans 5 Paul contrasts the two great rival ages, realms, or kingdoms, by contrasting Adam with Christ. The two great representative heads of humanity stand one against the other. As Thomas Goodwin puts it, 'There are but two men standing before God, Adam and Christ, and these two men have all other men hanging on their girdles.' Through Adam, the reign of death began, and extended to all his descendants, who sinned in him. But through Christ, the representative Head of the new humanity, life reigns and extends to all the elect in him. With the resurrection of Christ, the powers of darkness have for ever been shattered, and the 'age to come', or the kingdom of God, has come. To be in Christ, then, is to participate in the new creation. 'If anyone is in Christ, he is a new creation; the old has gone, the new has come' (2 Cor. 5:17). Just as death ruled in the old age of Adam, life rules in the new kingdom of Christ.

In chapters 5 to 8 Paul will demonstrate that to have life in Christ means to be free from the tyranny of the powers of destruction and darkness: wrath (ch. 5), sin (ch.6), law (ch. 7) and death (ch.8). In so doing he is simply demonstrating the implications of belonging to the kingdom of Christ.

Freedom from God's wrath (Romans 5)

Here Paul depicts the results of Christ's atonement with reference to God's holy anger, which man's sin incurred. The opening verse refers back to the grand theme of redemption which Paul has been expounding up to this point. 'Therefore, since we have been justified through faith...' The concluding verse of the chapter similarly declares that the triumph over judgement is 'through Jesus Christ our Lord'. This refrain indeed will be repeated at the close of each of the next three chapters.

Through the redemptive work of the Lord Jesus Christ, divine justice has been satisfied, a perfect substitute having paid the price of our redemption. The believer's sin has been covered, and he is no longer under God's terrible wrath and judgement. He is at peace with God, and God is at peace with him. 'The judge who was judicially hostile is now judicially reconciled.' The sinner who was excluded from fellowship with the holy God now has a right of access, and cause to rejoice in hope of the glory of God. The source of these blessings was the love of God, and the grounds the death of Christ. 'But God demonstrates his own love for us in this: while we were still sinners, Christ died for us' (5:8). Reconciliation has been effected, and the believer has been freed from God's wrath through Christ (5:9).

In verses 12-21 Paul declares, through the Adam-Christ parallel, how it is that condemnation under the destructive power of the wrath of God, which belonged to the old age, has been replaced, through God's gracious work for us in Christ, by righteousness in the life of the believer. Just as solidarity with Adam in his disobedience brought condemnation and death for all, so through the solidarity of the elect with Christ in his obedience and resurrection, life is assured for all who are in Christ.

The law of God was subservient to God's purpose of grace, to shut up the sinner under condemnation, that he might be constrained to look for grace which alone could bring him salvation (5:20-21). Paul thus includes the law of God as belonging to the old age of sin and death. He will do the same in chapter 7, and show that the law is incapable of justifying the sinner (7:1-6), or of sanctifying the believer (7:7-13).

Meanwhile let us rejoice in the glorious truths depicted in chapter 5. Here is the first great implication of the gospel of sovereign grace. The believer is removed from a position of craven fear under the awful judgement and condemnation of a holy God. And with regard to the future Day of Judgement, he need have no fear. 'Since we have now been justified by his blood, how much more shall we be saved from God's wrath through him!' (5:9). Well might we sing the beautiful hymn of Augustus Montague Toplady (1740-78):

From whence this fear and unbelief?
Hath not the Father put to grief
His spotless Son for me?
And will the righteous Judge of men
Condemn me for that debt of sin
Which, Lord, was charged on thee?

Complete atonement thou hast made,
And to the utmost thou hast paid
Whate'er thy people owed;
How then can wrath on me take place,
If sheltered in thy righteousness,
And sprinkled with thy blood?

If thou hast my discharge procured,
And freely in my room endured
The whole of wrath divine;
Payment God cannot twice demand,
First at my bleeding Surety's hand,
And then again at mine.

Turn then, my soul, unto thy rest!
The merits of thy great High Priest
Have bought thy liberty;
Trust in his efficacious blood,
Nor fear thy banishment from God,
Since Jesus died for thee.

Freedom from sin and law (Romans 6, 7)

These two chapters deal with questions which arise directly out of
Paul's teaching on justification by faith.

Chapter 5 brings to a climax Paul's exposition of justification by
faith. Through Christ, the reign of sin unto death has been
superseded by the reign of grace unto life. Though the offence
abounded, grace abounded much more. Thus God's righteousness
has been established by the gospel of grace.

This, however, raises two particular problems, both associated
with the question of law.

Firstly, does the fact that justification is provided by grace, rather
than being procured by law-keeping, not undermine *morality,* and
lead to antinomianism or lawlessness? Are we not justifying a
response such as that expressed in the phrase: 'Let us continue in sin
that grace may abound'? Are not the legalists right in claiming that
justification by grace, without the works of the law, is an absurdity?

Secondly, if justification is apart from law, have we not
undermined *law,* and diminished its value and usefulness? The
question here relates to the whole function and purpose of law in the
economy of redemption.

Paul answers the first question in chapter 6 by asserting that the
Christian is free from sin. Justification inevitably leads to
sanctification.

The second question is answered in chapter 7, where the apostle
asserts equally dogmatically that the Christian is free from the law.
Law neither justifies the sinner nor sanctifies the saint.

Free from sin (Romans 6)

The first great consequence of justification by faith, as we have
seen, is freedom from the wrath of God. The second great implication is holiness of life. Rather than undermining sanctification,
gratuitous pardon ensures that God's people are free from sin once
and for all.

Union with Christ

Through the solidarity of the elect with Christ, the believer is united
with Christ, his representative Head, both in his death and in his
resurrection. Already in chapter 5 Paul has stated that the whole
purpose of grace is to deliver us from the bondage and reign of sin,
and to put us under the reign of grace (5:20-21). This he explains
further in this chapter by presenting the believer's union with Christ
(6:1-14), and illustrating this with reference to slave-market
practice (6:15-23).

The antinomian charge that grace undermines morality is preposterous, for a Christian, through union with Christ, has died to sin
and been raised to a new life in Christ. He has been united with

Christ in his death, and also in his resurrection. His old self has been crucified with him, so that the body of sin might be rendered powerless. Through Christ we are free from sin's rule, dominion and power, and free to serve Christ. So in verse 11 the Christian is exhorted to appreciate the facts which obtain by virtue of union with Christ, and in verses 12-14 he is exhorted to live as one who has already entered the resurrection life: 'Therefore do not let sin reign in your mortal body!' Here the imperative flows from the indicative. As John Murray puts it, 'The presupposition of the exhortation is not that sin reigns but the opposite, that it does not reign, and it is for this reason that the exhortation can have validity and appeal.'[2] 'Sin shall not have dominion over you' (6:14, NKJV). This is not an exhortation, but a statement of assured fact. It is the conclusive proof that the antinomian assertion is false.

In verse 14 Paul explains why sin will not exercise its dominion, or mastery. It is because 'You are not under law, but under grace.' This statement is of particular interest because of its bearing on our study, the place of law in the doctrine of sanctification. Law, like sin, belongs to the old realm from which grace alone can deliver.

Slaves to righteousness

Paul further illustrates his claim that justification secures holiness rather than undermining it. If subjection to grace ensures our sanctification, so too does freedom from law. Slaves, he declares, serve their master with exclusive obedience. If there is an exchange of ownership, there is continued service, but to a different master. Now conversion involves a change of master. As unbelievers we once served sin (personified as a slave-owner), and our service led to death. Now, as believers, we serve an entirely different master, righteousness, and our service leads to life. Thus holiness of life is assured by the Christian being exclusively bound to his new master, righteousness. The old bondage to our old master, sin, led to service of a sort we are now ashamed to remember, things which result in death. The new service is totally different. It leads to holiness, and results in eternal life.

Both our union with Christ in death and resurrection and our change of mastery from law to grace, far from undermining morality, secure it.

Freed for conflict

This freedom from sin does not, however, exonerate the Christian from having to do battle with sin. The triumphant note of this chapter is not to be confused with presumptive triumphalism. If the decisive victory has been secured, local pockets of resistance from the remnants of the defeated army remain and must be eradicated. If the dominant note of this chapter is one of victory through Christ, there are clear references to spiritual conflict, which necessarily ensues. The person who has ceased from sin must as a consequence do battle against it. There is no room for quietism or pacifism here. Grace abounds, so he must not go on sinning (6:1). We have been crucified with Christ so that the body of sin might be rendered powerless, that we should no longer be slaves to sin (6:6). It is on the basis of the emancipating power of the gospel that the exhortations of verses 12 and 13 are founded: 'Therefore do not let sin reign in your mortal body so that you obey its evil desires. Do not offer the parts of your body to sin, as instruments of wickedness, but rather offer yourselves to God, as those who have been brought from death to life; and offer the parts of your body to him as instruments of righteousness. For sin shall not be your master, because you are not under law, but under grace.' Here the imperative is based on the indicative. We are called to be what we are, freed from sin. He who is not free from sin is not free to fight against it, for he is the slave of sin. But through Christ we have been emancipated from the enslaving power of sin, and as a result we engage in conflict against every pocket of resistance and manifestation of the vestiges of sin. The spiritual conflict we experience is the outworking of the gospel truth: 'Sin shall not be your master, because you are not under law, but under grace' (6:14).

The conflict, or tension, which here runs parallel with the triumph of the gospel, is significant in that this will be the theme in the latter half of chapter 7, in the context of the Christian's freedom from the law (7:14-25). There we read, 'In my inner being I delight in God's law; but I see another law at work in the members of my body, waging war against the law of my mind... What a wretched man I am! Who will rescue me from this body of death? Thanks be to God — through Jesus Christ our Lord!' (7:22-25).

The same conflict recurs in chapter 8, where the subject is the believer's freedom from death. 'Therefore, brothers, we have an obligation — but it is not to the sinful nature, to live according to it. For if you live according to the sinful nature, you will die; but if by the Spirit you put to death the misdeeds of the body, you will live.'

This is a strong indication that chapter 7:14-25 is correctly to be understood as depicting the depth of spiritual conflict encountered by those who have experienced the liberating power of the gospel from the tyranny of wrath, sin, law and death.

Freedom from law (Romans 7)

We come now to the chapter with which we are particularly concerned in this study. At this point we are especially interested in its setting in the epistle as a whole, before proceeding to examine in detail the text itself. In adopting this approach we are simply obeying one of the great principles of biblical interpretation, that is, paying regard to the context in which a passage is found. Untold error would be avoided if we observed this fundamental rule. If we isolate this chapter from the development of Paul's thought up to this point in the epistle, we are liable totally to misunderstand the passage, and to regard it as a mere restatement of his doctrine of justification by faith, a description of the inner turmoil of a sinner needing to be regenerated, or in process of being regenerated.

Two errors are to be avoided. The first is that of seeing the chapter as a parenthesis, unconnected with the theme of the epistle. We do violence to the text if we consider it a digression from Paul's concern in chapters 5 to 8 to describe the Christian life. Just as the subject of chapters 9 to 11, far from being a separate issue divorced from the central theme of the epistle, is intimately related to the question of the righteousness of God, so chapter 7 is intimately bound up with the unfolding theme of the epistle.

A second error to be avoided is that of considering the duality revealed in this chapter as personal or psychological, and of failing to recognize that the great backdrop of Paul's thought is the fact of two conflicting worlds or ages. The chapter does witness to conflict within the human heart, but it is not caused by some sort of personal psychological disunity or schizophrenia. Rather it reflects the eschatological tensions of the believer's dual position — in the world but not of it.

We must grasp the essential unity of the epistle, and understand the chapter in the context of chapters 5 to 8. Then we shall see that in chapter 7 Paul pursues his plan of demonstrating that those who are justified by faith live. His concern is not to present a personal biographical confession, nor to discuss a psychological dichotomy within man. The dualism which lies behind the personal expressions of tension and frustration within the chapter is the eschatological dualism which pervades the theology of Paul. This eschatological dualism is at the root of the dualism between flesh and spirit, earth and heaven, sin and justification. It is the dualism of the two reigns, the reign of law and the reign of Christ. Paul places the experience of being under law directly in contrast with being in Christ. This is because with the coming of the Messiah the new age has begun. The old principle of law, by which the Jew was bound to God, has been replaced by the new principle of participation in Christ by faith. In chapter 7 Paul is concerned to examine the role of the law in the economy of God, and its significance in the Christian life. His particular interest is not primarily personal and subjective, but objective, theological and practical.

There is great unity of thought throughout chapters 5 to 8. Paul is declaring that through the work of Christ the believer is freed from the tyrannical powers which ruled under the old realm — wrath, sin, law and death. Divine grace in Christ, ministered to us by the Holy Spirit, ensures a life of holiness. Chapter 7, then, is intimately related to what immediately precedes it, and to what immediately follows it.

The role of the law in the economy of God

Having dealt in turn with the two regnant evil powers of wrath (ch. 5), and sin (ch. 6), the apostle now takes up the discussion of the law, and declares in chapter 7 that the Christian is free from the law. He has already stated this fact in the previous chapter (6:14). There he gave as ground of assurance that sin would not exercise dominion over the believer the fact that he was 'not under law, but under grace'. But he did not pause to explain what he meant by asserting that the believer is not under law. Rather he proceeded to illustrate the Christian's change of master, from sin to righteousness.

Clearly Paul is aware of the shock which 6:14 might produce in the minds of his readers. How surprising to find the law listed among the powers of destruction! He therefore deliberately returns to this point and elaborates it in chapter 7. He defines the role of the law in the two contrasting realms, the old age of sin and the new age of grace. In his discussion he does three things: Firstly he declares that *the law belongs to the old realm,* and is closely associated with the reigns of sin and death from which the believer is redeemed through Christ. Secondly, he declares that *the law,* despite its divine origin and great usefulness in many respects, *is unable to justify the sinner.* Finally, he declares that, similarly, *the law is unable to sanctify the believer.* The Spirit alone is able to do that, in virtue of the atoning work of Christ.

The law belongs to the old realm (7:1-6)

For Paul, legalism and grace are utterly incompatible. He does not hesitate to identify the law of God with the old realm of sin and death, despite its divine origin.

There are two passages which throw light on what Paul is saying here. In Galatians 4:1-6 Paul in similar fashion links the sinful passions and God's law. Galatians was written to combat the legalistic teaching of the Judaizers, who believed that salvation was ultimately dependent on keeping the law of God. Paul counters their error by emphasizing that grace emancipates from the servitude of the law: 'What I am saying is that as long as the heir is a child, he is no different from a slave, although he owns the whole estate. He is subject to guardians and trustees until the time set by his father. So also, when we were children, we were *in slavery under the basic principles of the world.* But when the time had fully come, God sent his Son, born of a woman, born under law, *to redeem those under law,* that we might receive the full rights of sons. Because you are sons, God sent the Spirit of his Son into our hearts, the Spirit who calls out, "Abba, Father." So you are no longer a slave, but a son; and since you are a son, God has made you also an heir.' Paul speaks similarly elsewhere in the same epistle: 'Did you receive the Spirit by observing the law, or by believing what you heard?' (Gal. 3:2). 'All who rely on observing the law are under a curse... Clearly no one is justified before God by the law, because, "The righteous will live by faith"... Christ redeemed us from the *curse of the law* by becoming a curse for us... so that by faith we might receive the promise of the Spirit' (Gal. 3:10-14). 'It is for freedom that Christ has set us free. Stand firm, then, and do not let yourselves be burdened again by a yoke of slavery' (Gal. 5:1).

Throughout Galatians Paul places law and grace in strong antithesis. The purpose for which God sent Christ into the world was precisely to liberate those who until then had been held captive under law, so that slavery might give way to sonship and receipt of the Spirit. For that reason the Judaizers were to be resisted strenuously, for their teaching enslaved men. The Christian is free from the law through Christ. If we continue in bondage to the law, we are still under the wrath of God, and belong to the old realm. But as those who have been justified we are not under law but under grace.

In a second passage, 1 Corinthians 15:56, Paul explains the intimate relationship which exists between the law and its allied powers of destruction, sin and death. 'The sting of death is sin, and the power of sin is the law. But thanks be to God! He gives us the victory through our Lord Jesus Christ.' Here the apostle asserts that what ultimately enables sin to perform its deadly work is the strength and dominion of the law. Clearly a legal spirit never emancipates. The law is powerless apart from the work of divine grace or the divine Spirit.

This theme of the impotence of the law is precisely Paul's subject in Romans 7. The law is powerless both to justify the sinner and to sanctify the believer. In the first six verses the Christian's freedom from the power of the law is illustrated from *marriage*. The power of any law over a person ceases with death. Take the simple illustration from marriage. During her lifetime, a wife is bound to her husband, but on his death she is released from the law of marriage, and is free to remarry. In a similar way, believers have been freed from the law by death, for through the body of Christ the Christian has been freed from the old relationship to *the law,* in order that now he might be united to the risen *Christ.* Now united to the living Christ, we are free to bring forth fruit — to live holy lives — for God. In our old carnal life, the sinful passions, excited by the law, made us bring forth fruit unto death. Now that we are delivered from it, we can serve God in a new way, the way of the Spirit, and not the old way of the written code.

In verses 4-6 Paul does not apply the illustration in a strictly logical way, for it is the believer, who died to the law, who is now free to be married to Christ. But the lesson Paul wants to establish is clear: legal obligation is terminated by death. He refrains from saying that the law died. Nowhere in Scripture is it said that the moral law of God has been repealed, or annulled, or put to death. The law is a transcript of God's character, so since God is eternally unchanging, we must not be surprised to discover that the expression of his holy will for his people is unchangeable. The point Paul makes is that we have been discharged from the law. There cannot be release in precisely the same form as in the illustration from marriage. But nevertheless there is a death which releases the bond as decisively as the death of the husband in the other case — and that death is our death to the law in the death of Christ. This is the definitive dissolution corresponding to the death of the husband in the marriage analogy.

Paul in verse 4 shows the way in which grace, in contrast to law, ensures our deliverance from the dominion of sin. As long as law governs us there is no possibility of release from the bondage of sin. The only alternative is discharge from the law. This occurs through our union with Christ in his death, because all the virtues of Christ's death in meeting the claims of the law become ours, and we are free from the bond-service and power of sin to which the law had consigned us. But discharge from the law is not an end in itself; it is directed to a positive end — the bearing of fruit unto God. Union with Christ in his death is paralleled by union with him in his resurrection. Thus grace reigning in Christ liberates us from slavery to the law, and 'dissolves our marriage-obligation to the law, thereby leaving us at liberty to contract a new relation — to be joined to the Risen One, in order to spiritual fruitfulness, to the glory of God'.[3] This deliverance from the law is not obtained by setting the law aside, or by disregarding its demands, but by those demands being satisfied in the person of Christ.

In verses 5 and 6 Paul announces his themes for the rest of the chapter. In verse 5 he describes the condition and experience of the old pre-Christian life, dominated by the sinful nature, under the reign of law, bringing forth fruit unto death. This will be his theme in verses 7-13: the inability of the law to justify the sinner.

In verse 6 he describes the experience of the believer who, released from the tyranny of law, is now free to serve in the new way of the Spirit, in the new state of mind of which the Holy Spirit is the author, and not in the old way of the written code (Gal. 3:3; 2 Cor. 3-6). This will be his theme in verses 14-25: the inability of the law to sanctify the believer.

The theme, then, of chapter 7 is freedom from the law. Just as union with Christ in his death and resurrection ensures freedom from sin (ch. 6), so believers are liberated through Christ from legalism. The consequence of this freedom is the service of God, in contrast to indulgence of sin.

Throughout the rest of the chapter Paul discusses the role and function of the law in the spiritual life, firstly in relation to his past unconverted state (7:7-13), then in relation to his life as a Christian (7:14-25).

The role of the law in the old world-order:
law cannot justify the sinner (7:7-13)

In these verses Paul demonstrates that while the law is incapable of making a bad man good, it has a positive role to play in the divine method of justification. Paul is replying to possible criticism that what he has written might appear to imply a depreciation of the law, as being in itself evil. He has identified the state of being 'under law' with that of being 'under sin' (6:14; 7:5). He has shown that sin's rule is exercised through the law (5:20;7:5). Does that not imply that the law is sin? (7:7). Paul emphatically rejects such a suggestion, and proceeds to present a clear statement depicting the function of the law in the gracious economy of God. His aim is to vindicate the law, and exonerate it from all blame. He makes three main points.

Firstly, the purpose of the law is to *expose sin,* and make sinners conscious of their sinful state. It does this not in an abstract and philosophical fashion, but in a personal way, and in concrete terms of conviction of particular transgressions.

Secondly, the law gives this knowledge of sin by *declaring God's prohibitions and commands.* Thereby the depravity residing within us is aroused to activity, is goaded into active rebellion and thus renders us conscious of our sinfulness, from which we need redemption. The law in this sense actually becomes the occasion of sin, just as a 'no smoking' sign can draw from an inveterate smoker a desire to reach for his cigarettes. But the law is not sinful. Its effect in practice, however, because of the sinfulness of the human heart, is to condemn, and for that reason it takes its place among the powers of destruction. 'I found that the very commandment that was intended to bring life actually brought death' (7:10).

Thirdly, the law *gives no ability to perform the good which it requires,* and cannot deliver from sin's guilt (7:9-11) or power (7:22-24). Paul summarizes this in verse 13: 'Did that which is good, then, become death to me? By no means! But in order that sin might be recognized as sin, it produced death in me through what was good, so that through the command sin might become utterly sinful.'

In making these points Paul seems to have in mind the narrative of the fall of Adam in Genesis. He has already referred to Adam's transgression of God's commandment in 5:14, and has related it to man's experience of sin against the law of Moses. Now in chapter 7 he speaks specifically of the sin of covetousness (7:7). Covetousness is the archetypal sin, the setting of the heart on evil things (1 Cor. 10:6), so that other sins are merely the expression of this fundamental sin. The essence of Adam's sin was covetousness, and this sin was later codified in the tenth commandment. For that reason Paul here illustrates the relation between law and sin by referring to the primeval and essential sin of covetousness.

He presents his view in a highly personal way, by speaking in the first person singular. Sin is no abstract principle of which the apostle has no personal experience. There is nothing hypocritical here. The personal references add vividness and conviction to the truths the apostle is expounding. 'Sin ... produced in me every kind of covetous desire... I found that the very commandment that was intended to bring life actually brought death... For sin ... deceived me, and through the commandment put me to death... In order that sin might be recognized as sin, it produced death in me through what was good, so that through the commandment sin might become utterly sinful.'

These personal references must not mask the fact that there is more here than personal autobiography. Paul is making dogmatic affirmations of an objective nature, and laying down principles which have a universal relevance. The Adam motif which seems to lie behind his personal references, while not dealt with in a detailed and reasoned manner, indicates that he thinks of his own experiences as a typical and representative experience. He draws from his own experience universally valid conclusions.

Paul is writing from the perspective of a regenerate man. He looks back through the eyes of faith, with all the insights of a believer, to his unregenerate days when he experienced slavery to sin. He does so, not to reminisce, but to demonstrate that the true function of the law is to detect, excite, expose and condemn sin in the unbeliever. The main theme of this chapter is, as we have said, the function of the law, and in verses 7-13 he poignantly and graphically illustrates its inability to justify the sinner.

Verses 7-13 are an expansion of the scene depicted in verse 5: 'When we were controlled by the sinful nature, the sinful passions aroused by the law were at work in our bodies, so that we bore fruit for death.' But Paul is able to exonerate the law of God from any blame by illustrating from his own experience the guilt of his own heart in the whole process of sin.

We do well to recognize the importance of this great truth. Man in sin is ever ready to shift the blame for his sinfulness, just as Adam sought to incriminate Eve and the serpent that beguiled him. But he is held responsible for his own sin. In addition there is the fatal tendency in the sinner to try to acquire personal righteousness on the basis of law-keeping. That was the essence of Pharisaism. But the law always penetrates our feeble disguises, exposes our sin and condemns us. This it does because it is a transcript of the righteous demands of a holy God. The law can never justify a sinner; rather, by stirring up man's uncontrollable covetousness, it fixes man's feet more firmly on the road of death.

Paul has come to recognize sin through the law. He does not say that he would not have been a sinner without the law, but that he would not have known sin as he now knows it, or have seen himself to be a sinner (3:20). 'The knowledge is not merely theoretical knowledge respecting the nature and fact of sin but the practical experimental conviction that he himself was sinful. The law convicted him of his own sin and sinfulness.'[4] Clearly the law of God exemplified in the Ten Commandments, particularly the tenth one which strikes at the whole fallen nature of man, was the one used by the Holy Spirit to convince him of his sin and guilt, and to drive him to look for forgiveness through divine grace. How futile it is to seek salvation on the basis of obedience to the law, for no one is able perfectly to obey it! 'There is no one righteous, not even one... There is no one who does good, not even one... Therefore no one will be declared righteous in his sight by observing the law: rather through the law we become conscious of sin' (3:10,12,20). All the law can do is expose sin, awaken sin, condemn the sinner and shut him up to his desperate plight, from which grace alone can deliver him. But, thanks be to God, grace is extended to sinners in the glorious gospel of the Lord Jesus Christ!

Horatius Bonar (1808-89) was well aware of the law's inability to justify the sinner when he penned these beautiful verses:

Not what these hands have done
Can save this guilty soul;
Not what this toiling flesh has borne
Can make my spirit whole.

Not what I feel or do
Can give me peace with God;
Not all my prayers, and sighs, and tears
Can bear my awful load.

Thy work alone, O Christ,
Can ease this weight of sin;
Thy blood alone, O Lamb of God,
Can give me peace within.

Thy love to me, O God,
Not mine, O Lord, to thee
Can rid me of this dark unrest,
And set my spirit free.

Thy grace alone, O God,
To me can pardon speak;
Thy power alone, O Son of God,
Can this sore bondage break.

I bless the Christ of God,
I rest on love divine,
And with unfaltering lip and heart,
I call this Saviour mine.

In another beautiful hymn Isaac Watts (1674-1748) expresses the response of faith, on the part of a guilty sinner, to the call of the gospel:

How sad our state of nature is!
Our sin how deep it stains:
And Satan binds our captive minds
Fast in his slavish chains.

But there's a voice of sovereign grace
Sounds from the sacred word—
Ho! ye despairing sinners, come,
And trust upon the Lord.

My soul obeys the almighty call,
And runs to this relief;
I would believe thy promise, Lord;
Oh, help my unbelief!

To the dear fountain of thy blood,
Incarnate God, I fly;
Here let me wash my guilty soul
From crimes of deepest dye.

A guilty, weak and helpless wretch,
On thy kind arms I fall;
Be thou my strength and righteousness,
My Jesus and my all.

The role of the law in the life of the believer:
law cannot sanctify the believer (7:14-25)

It is clear that Paul does not here embark upon a new topic. His
subject is still the law of God, its function and purpose in the
economy of God. He continues to speak in terms of human
experience, indeed of his own personal experience as representative
of others. But now he speaks of his experience *as a believer* and
depicts his utter frustration on discovering that just as the law could
not justify him when he was an unregenerate sinner, neither can it
sanctify him now that he is a believer. But frustration is not the last
word. Even as he depicts the inability of the law to lead to holiness,
he thanks God that the day will come when through the Lord Jesus
Christ he will be rescued from the body of death.

In these verses Paul is showing how the law gives the knowledge of sin which remains within him, even though he is a child of God. When he examines his life in the light of God's law, he always finds that he has done less than the good that he wanted to do. Thus he finds that sin is still in him, and that he is still to a degree taken captive by it (7:20-23). This is not, of course, the totality of a believer's experience. The great blessings communicated through the gospel will be set out in chapter 8. It is, however, what is revealed to the heart of a believer by the law. The wretchedness of the wretched man thus springs from the discovery of his continuing sinfulness, and the knowledge that he cannot hope to be rid of indwelling sin while he remains in the body. He longs for deliverance from the presence of sin, but is painfully conscious that for the present his reach exceeds his grasp. He longs therefore for the eschatological deliverance which will be his one day, on the day of Christ's revelation in glory. Then, and only then, will the tension between his desire and his achievement be abolished.

The hymn-writer well expresses this longing:

Keep us, Lord, oh, keep us cleaving
To thyself and still believing,
Till the hour of our receiving
Promised joys in heaven.

Then we shall be where we would be,
Then we shall be what we should be,
That which is not now, nor could be,
Then shall be our own.

(Thomas Kelly, 1769-1855).

Meanwhile Paul the believer groans under the burden of continuing imperfection, and expresses his grief at his discovery of the relics of sin in his life, as God's holy law exposes it. 'I am unspiritual [or carnal], sold as a slave to sin' (7:14). 'So then, I myself in my mind am a slave to God's law, but in the sinful nature a slave to the law of sin' (7:25).

His aspirations after perfection will be re-echoed in chapter 8, where Paul declares, 'We ... who have the first-fruits of the Spirit, groan inwardly as we wait eagerly for our adoption as sons, the redemption of our bodies' (8:23).

Six supporting arguments

This view of verses 14 to 25, which I have called the Reformed view, is much more satisfactory than those which view the passage as depicting the state of lostness of an unregenerate man, or the plight of an 'unsanctified saint', or a sinner in the throes of experiencing conviction of sin. It enables us to account for various features in the text itself, and for the setting of the paragraph in the epistle.

Firstly, it accounts naturally for the change from past to present tense which we find from verse 14 onwards. Already, just before commencing his section on the ministry of the law, Paul spoke of what we once were (7:5), and of what we henceforth are as Christians (7:6). There he seems to have given an outline of what is to follow. Verses 7-13 are all in the past tense, and refer to Paul's experience before his conversion. Verses 14-25 are all in the present tense. The natural way to understand this section is to see it as descriptive of Paul's experience at the time of writing. The suggestion that Paul is in fact commenting on his past experience, referred to in verses 7-13, and that he uses the present tense merely for the sake of vividness, is unconvincing. There is no comparison with the use by the evangelists of the historic present tense in the Gospel narratives to give vividness. Here we do not have narrative, but generalized explanatory comment. We have no right to ignore what the text actually says.

Secondly, the Reformed view presented above fits the general context in which the passage is found. Throughout chapters 5-8 Paul is dealing with the meaning of the Christian life. Having shown the inability of the law to justify sinners, he proceeds to show its utter powerlessness to carry on the work of sanctification, even in the heart of renewed men, thus warning them against a spirit of legalism. If in verses 14-25 Paul again describes the situation of an unregenerate person this would be a case of useless repetition.

Thirdly, the Reformed view naturally accounts for Paul's conclusion at the end of the chapter: 'So then, I myself in my mind am a slave to God's law, but in the sinful nature a slave to the law of sin' (7:25). Those who understand the passage as referring to a state of sinfulness from which unredeemed humanity needs to be rescued through Christ find it impossible to fit this sentence into their scheme. It is a shattering and inexplicable anticlimax to the apostle's triumphant declaration of deliverance at the beginning of verse 25. The Reformed view outlined above accounts perfectly for the inference of the second part of verse 25. It is a summary of the Christian's inward struggle against sin which, though defeated, continues to manifest itself in his life.

Fourthly, the Reformed view naturally accounts for statements describing Paul's natural affinity with the law of God revealed in his approving it (7:16), delighting in it (7:22), wishing to fulfil it (7:15,18-21) and serving it with his mind and in his inner being (7:22-25). If we adopt the position that the passage refers to an unregenerate person, it is difficult to make sense of these statements. According to this view, Paul would then be speaking of a man in Adam as having a natural affinity with the law of God, something which elsewhere he consistently denies. This is clearly asserted in the next chapter, where in the opening paragraph Paul declares, 'Those who live according to the flesh set their minds on the things of the flesh ... the carnal mind is enmity against God; for it is not subject to the law of God, nor indeed can be' (8:5,7, NKJV). According to this statement, Paul in verses 14-25 of chapter 7 could not possibly be describing a man in Adam, but only a man in Christ.

Fifthly, the Reformed view naturally accounts for the cry of the 'wretched man' for deliverance from the body of this death, that is, from this mortal body which is at present sin's place of residence. This redemption of the body will come at the final consummation of God's purposes, a consummation for which, according to chapter 8:23, those who have the Spirit wait, groaning.

Finally, the Reformed position accounts for the tension within the apostle's experience. This tension has nothing to do with a discordant and divided state of the soul, a psychological dualism or spiritual schizophrenia. Throughout this chapter Paul is discussing the meaning and position of the law. The duality and tensions revealed are caused by the tension which exists in the Christian life between will and action, between aspirations and achievements. This results from the believer's double status as one who, on the one hand, belongs to Christ and to the new world-order and yet, on the other, because, he is still in this world and in the flesh, belongs to some degree to the old world-order. The conflict is the result of his double situation in the two world-orders. It is this dualism which constrains Paul to aspire after total eschatological deliverance in verse 25. His cry is not one of despair, but of frustration and longing, as he groans, waiting for the redemption of the body. With assured

confidence he can go on to express thanksgiving: 'I thank God —
through Jesus Christ our Lord.' Through Christ the victory is
already won, so that we may look forward with confidence to the day
of full and final redemption.

When we approach the passage from the Reformed view
outlined above, the meaning of Paul's cry is seen to be entirely
consistent with the experience of the Christian as depicted in the
chapter as a whole.

Freedom from death (Romans 8)

In this glorious chapter Paul reaches the climax of his argument, and
declares in glowing terms the believer's certain triumph over sin and
its ultimate power, death.

While he introduces the theme with startling abruptness, it
comes naturally and logically as the conclusion of the argument he
has been presenting through the preceding chapters. Having shown
that we are justified gratuitously, that is by grace through faith,
without the works of the law, he has proceeded to demonstrate that
the believer is free from the tyranny of sin and law. He has shown
by referring to his own personal experience that the law is as
incapable of sanctifying the saint as it is of justifying the sinner. He
has presented one aspect of the believer's present experience, his
distress and groanings as he longs for total and perfect deliverance
from the remnants of sin which, through the agency of the law, he
finds within his members. But this is only one aspect of Christian
experience. Chapter 8 completes the picture by describing the
deliverance he experiences in this life through the Spirit, and the
total victory over his final enemy, death, which awaits him in Christ.

The shadow of this last enemy, death, has lain across the last three
chapters of Romans. In chapter 5, the Adam-Christ passage went on to
depict the contrast between the dominion of death and the dominion of
life. In chapter 6, where the tyrant under discussion was sin, Paul
showed that bondage to sin ends finally in death. In chapter 7, where
the main topic was man's thraldom to the law, the 'wretched man'
yearned to be rescued from the body of death and rejoiced that this was
guaranteed 'through Jesus Christ our Lord'. Now, in the eighth chapter,
Paul deals separately with the Christian's freedom from the tyranny of
the fourth and final enemy, death.

The chapter divides naturally into three sections. In the first seventeen verses the theme is *life through the Spirit*. The Christian life is characterized by the indwelling of God's Spirit, who frees us from death that we might have life. The theme in the second section, verses 18-25, is the *future glory*. Our present sufferings are contrasted with the glory of the age to come. Finally, in the third section, verses 28-39, the topic is encapsulated in the phrase *'more than conquerors'*. Here we find the conclusion of the foregoing argument of the epistle. Full and final triumph is guaranteed for the believer through Jesus Christ our Lord.

In Romans 8 Paul is unquestionably describing the experience of a believer. He is speaking of 'those who are in Christ Jesus', who have been 'set ... free from the law of sin and death' (8:1), who 'do not live according to the sinful nature but according to the Spirit' (8:4). They 'have their minds set on what the Spirit desires' (8:5), and the Spirit of God lives in them (8:9). They have the first-fruits of the Spirit, and groan inwardly as they eagerly anticipate the redemption of the body (8:23). Their final glorification is assured, for God is for them (8:31).

The great characteristic of the people under discussion in this chapter is that they live their lives in accordance with the Spirit of God. He indwells them and is the controlling force in their lives. There are some twenty references to the Spirit in this single chapter, whereas the term is found only five times in the first seven chapters. The theme of this chapter, then, is the spiritual life of the believer and the glorification that awaits him.

But the references to law are equally significant. Since we have been freely justified by faith in Christ, and are indwelt and enabled by the Holy Spirit, 'The righteous requirements of the law [are] fully met in us, who do not live according to the sinful nature but according to the Spirit' (8:4). Through the Spirit the law of God is established and fulfilled in the life of the believer, even during the period while he awaits his future glorification.

Unity of thought between chapters 7 and 8

We must be careful not to over-emphasize the contrast between chapters 7 and 8. The chapter divisions are unnatural and may hide the continuity of thought between the last section of chapter 7 (vv.

14-25) and chapter 8. Paul is describing in both the same experience, though from different perspectives.

In chapter 7 Paul has been opening his heart to describe truly Christian experience in the discovery of the sinfulness of his heart as he progresses in holiness. He had found remaining sin most troublesome. Rather than a denial of his spirituality, this was a true mark of spiritual sensitivity and an enlightened conscience. Any advance towards spiritual maturity is marked by an increased sense of the loathsomeness of sin, increased conflict with sin and an increased longing after full and final deliverance, represented in the redemption of the body. This fact is beautifully portrayed in the following poem by John Newton (1725-1807):

I asked the Lord that I might grow
In faith, and love, and every grace,
Might more of his salvation know,
And seek more earnestly his face.

'Twas he who taught me thus to pray,
And he, I trust, has answered prayer;
But it has been in such a way
As almost drove me to despair.

I hoped that in some favoured hour
At once he'd answer my request;
And, by his love's constraining power,
Subdue my sins, and give me rest.

Instead of this, he made me feel
The hidden evils of my heart,
And let the angry powers of hell
Assault my soul in very part.

Yea, more, with his own hand he seemed
Intent to aggravate my woe,
Crossed all the fair designs I schemed,
Blasted my gourds, and laid me low.

'Lord, why is this?' I trembling cried,
'Wilt thou pursue thy worm to death?'

''Tis in this way', the Lord replied,
'I answer prayer for grace and faith.

'These inward trials I employ,
From self and pride to set thee free,
And break thy schemes of earthly joy,
That thou mayest seek thy all in me.'

It is a sad reflection on the shallowness of much of contemporary evangelicalism that we find it difficult to identify this discovery of the hidden evils of the heart with authentic Christian experience. Wherever the Holy Spirit is present in a human heart, he provokes conflict with sin. The more there is of the Spirit's ministry in our hearts, the more will the depths of inbred sin be discovered, and the greater will be the resultant spiritual conflict.

While it is true that in these particular verses in chapter 7 the Holy Spirit is not explicitly mentioned, his activity is everywhere apparent. How else can we account for the fact that Paul delights in God's law in his inner being (7:22), that he can describe himself in his mind as a 'slave to God's law' (7:25), that he ardently desires to do what is good (7:18) and rejoices that one day he will be rescued 'from this body of death' through Jesus Christ his Lord?

In these verses Paul is setting forth the discoveries made to his regenerate heart by the law of God. If the experience is one of conflict and aspiration, that is because that is all the law of God can contribute. Chapter 8 describes the same Christian life from a different perspective. This is just one more aspect of the sanctifying work of divine grace.

The twin experiences of chapters 7 and 8 are to be viewed concurrently, not consecutively. E. F. Kevan presents the dual experience of the Christian succinctly when he writes, 'There is no question of an experimental "moving on" here from Romans 7 into Romans 8. The *argument* moves on, it is true, but the *experience* with which the two chapters are concerned is the one and the same sanctifying work of the Holy Spirit. Romans 8 takes the exposition forward, and describes the all-sufficiency of the life of the indwelling Spirit of God; but the experimental knowledge of this will mean for the believer an increasing discovery of the depths of sinful corruption in his heart — a discovery that ever keeps pace with true advance in holiness. "Oh, wretched man that I *am*!" is precisely the language which the apostle as a highly spiritual man might be expected to use. It will ever be the estimate that the sanctified believer makes of himself. The more sanctified a man is, the more will he acknowledge the wretchedness of his own heart. This is the saving work of the Holy Spirit: this is the deepening conviction of sin without which no man shall be sanctified.'[5]

The intimate connection between the two chapters becomes particularly clear if, with Murray, Bruce and Hendriksen, we understand 'condemnation' in the first verse of chapter 8 to refer not to forensic judgement, God's judicial sentence on sin, but to the penal servitude that follows judgement. If 'condemnation' were simply the opposite of 'justification', Paul would be saying that those who are in Christ Jesus are justified; but that stage of the argument was reached in chapter 3:21. According to Arndt-Gingrich, the word 'condemnation' here means 'probably not "condemnation" but the punishment following sentence' — in other words, 'penal servitude'. There is no reason why those in Christ Jesus should go on doing penal servitude to sin as though they had never been pardoned and never been liberated from the prison-house of sin. Murray argues strongly that the context supports such a view. Paul 'is not dealing with justification and the expiatory aspect of Christ's work but with sanctification and with what God has done in Christ to deliver us from the power of sin'.[6] It is a question of liberation from sin's power rather than from its guilt. In chapter 8, then, Paul is restating his glorious response to his agonizing cry of chapter 7:24. In Christ Jesus victory, full and final, is assured in this life and the life to come.

Another clear point of contact between chapters 7 and 8, which seems to confirm the view of the experiences of chapter 7 and 8 as being twin, concurrent experiences of conflict and victory, is the assurance of future glory expressed in verses 18-27. In the first seventeen verses Paul has shown how, through Christ, we have been removed from the power of sin and death, and given new life. But present human experience and the constant menace of death would seem to deny that. Paul resolves this tension by pointing to the coming glory: 'I consider that our present sufferings are not worth comparing with the glory that will be revealed in us' (8:18). The suffering itself is a preparation for glory (2 Cor. 4:17). In the age to come, the tension and conflict which have marked our Christian life in the world will be resolved. As Nygren puts it, 'The victory of life over death has already been won. Therefore this present life with all its infirmity reaches ahead, with sighs and yearnings, towards the final manifestation of the glory.'

This is very similar to the cry of the wretched man in 7:24 for deliverance 'from this body of death', that is, this mortal body, which is at present sin's place of residence. The groanings and longings which in 7:24 are expressed in deeply personal terms are here presented on a cosmic scale. In chapter 8 the whole cosmos shares in this longing: 'The whole creation has been groaning as in the pains of childbirth right up to the present time. Not only so, but we ourselves, who have the first-fruits of the Spirit, groan inwardly as we wait eagerly for our adoption as sons, the redemption of our bodies' (8:22-23). The Spirit himself groans and intercedes for the day of fulfilment, when all God's purposes will be consummated.

In verses 28-29 Paul widens the perspective to its fullest dimension, and exults in the certainty of complete victory over all our enemies, even death itself: 'We are more than conquerors through him who loved us' (8:37). Just as the personal longings of chapter 7 are echoed and widened in chapter 8, so too the shout of triumph of verse 25 is taken up and developed to include final, consummate victory.

It seems clear, then, that the Reformed view of Romans 7 is entirely consistent with its setting in the first eight chapters of the epistle.

3.
Spirit-provoked conflict

A careful study of the text itself confirms the view that Paul, in the second section of Romans 7, depicts in his person the conflicts within the heart of a child of God. Sometimes we pray that God would quicken our spiritual sensitivity, that we might discover the extent and degree to which sin remains within us:

Throw light into the darkened cells
Where passion reigns within:
Quicken my conscience till it feels
The loathsomeness of sin.

Search all my thoughts, the secret springs,
The motives that control:
The chambers where polluted things
Hold empire o'er the soul.

Ernest Kevan makes the comment: 'To make prayers such as these will bring us increasingly to the place where we cry, "Oh, wretched man that I am!"' When Paul wrote these words he 'sounded the highest note of sanctified experience this side of heaven'. As we consider the sacred text, may we experience something of the Spirit's ministry in our hearts!

'We know that the law is spiritual, but I am unspiritual [carnal], sold as a slave to sin' (7:14).

Paul is explaining the inability of the law to produce any good. His answer is direct and clear: the fault does not lie in the law, but in man himself. The law is spiritual; it is my own heart which is carnal, or unspiritual.

Two things might surprise us in this statement: firstly, that Paul speaks of the law as spiritual, since grace and law are often presented as contradictory principles; secondly, that he could describe a Christian as carnal.

The spirituality of the law

The law is consistently spoken of in Scripture as spiritual, despite the fact that in Christ we are free from the law (7:6). We are dead to the law as a means of righteousness (Gal. 2:19). We are redeemed from its curse (Gal. 3:13). It has been abolished, as a ceremonial system (Matt. 27:51). Nevertheless God's law continues to exercise a positive spiritual function. It gives to sinners the knowledge of sin (Rom. 3:20), and thus has a vital role in evangelism. But its function does not stop with conversion. It continues to exercise a ministry in the life of the believer, who is obligated to obey the commandments of God. The child of God is still under the moral law.

When Paul states that the law is spiritual he has in mind not only its divine origin, but also its divine authority and character, and the nature of its influence in the heart of the believer.

The law is spiritual because it was given by inspiration of the Holy Spirit. Peter affirms this when he writes, 'Prophecy never had its origin in the will of man, but men spoke from God as they were carried along by the Holy Spirit' (2 Peter 1:21; see also Matt. 22:43; Mark 12:36; Acts 1:16; 4:25; 28:25). It is for this reason authoritative, bearing all the sanctions of its divine Author. Being spiritual, it cannot properly be understood without the help of the same Spirit by whom it was given (1 Cor. 2:10-16). It is only those who have the Spirit who can profit from the law. They acknowledge the law, consent to it with their minds (Rom. 7:16,22,23,25) and obey it (8:1). Those who do not have the Spirit might well concern themselves with the letter of the law (7:6), but the letter without the Spirit kills (2 Cor. 3:6).

The Holy Spirit, by means of the law of God, exercises a spiritual ministry in the human heart. Scripture consistently speaks of such a ministry. In 1 Chronicles it is stated: 'The Lord searches every heart and understands every motive behind the thoughts' (1 Chron. 28:9). Such a ministry is particularly evident in Psalm 139:

'O Lord, you have searched me
    and you know me...
You perceive my thoughts from afar...
Where can I go from your Spirit?
    Where can I flee from your presence?...
Search me, O God, and know my heart;
    test me and know my anxious thoughts.
See if there is any offensive way in me,
    and lead me in the way everlasting'

(Ps. 139:1,2,7,23-24).

Psalm 119 indicates that the Spirit normally exercises his ministry towards us through God's Word, the law of God:

'I am laid low in the dust;
    preserve my life according to your word.
I recounted my ways and you answered me;
    teach me your decrees.
Let me understand the teaching of your precepts;
    then I will meditate on your wonders'

(Ps. 119:25-27).

Paul confidently declares in Romans 7:14 that all believers have personal experience of the spirituality of the law. It is this fact which makes the subsequent revelation of conflict and burden understandable. So long as someone regards the law as a rule extending to outward conduct only, he might well consider himself 'blameless', or 'alive'. That was Paul's experience before he was converted. The regenerate heart, however, recognizes that the law is 'holy, righteous and good' (7:12-13), that it comes from God, and by his Spirit penetrates to the secret desires of the heart, 'even to dividing soul and spirit, joints and marrow; it judges the thoughts and attitudes of the heart. Nothing in all creation is hidden from God's sight. Everything is uncovered and laid bare before the eyes of him to whom we must give account' (Heb. 4:12-13). This being so, the believer is all too conscious of his deep sinfulness and longs for holiness.

Haldane comments, 'Perceiving, then, that it [the law] requires truth in the inward parts, piercing even to the dividing asunder of soul and spirit, not only prohibiting the smallest outward deviation from holiness, but detecting every hidden ambush of the deceitful heart, Paul the Apostle, a man of like passion with ourselves, exclaims, "I am carnal, sold under sin." He here begins to declare his present experience, and changes the past time for the present, in which he continues afterwards to speak to the end of the chapter.'[1]

In 2 Corinthians 3 Paul contrasts law and Spirit, and draws attention to the consequences of understanding the law carnally rather than spiritually. 'Our competence comes from God. He has made us competent as ministers of a new covenant — not of the letter but of the Spirit; for the letter kills, but the Spirit gives life' (2 Cor. 3:6). The mistake made by the Jews was to regard the letter only, to take a carnal view of the law. That was the 'veil' that still covered their faces, and blinded their understanding. But the Christian, or regenerate, view is that the law is spiritual, and is as much concerned about motives and desires as it is about actions.

What Paul says in Romans 7:14 echoes what he has already stated earlier in the chapter regarding the believer: 'So, my brothers, you also died to the law through the body of Christ, that you might belong to another... But now, by dying to what once bound us, we have been released from the law so that we serve in the new way of the Spirit, and not in the old way of the written code' (7:4,6).

It is against this understanding of the law as spiritual that Paul goes on to speak of the sinfulness of his own regenerate heart. The law is given by God, is an expression of his holy will and is spiritual. But as the law is impotent to produce righteousness and life within the heart of the unbeliever, so it is impotent to produce holiness in the heart of the believer. The fault, however, does not belong to the law; rather it is due to man's sinful and carnal state.

The 'carnal' Christian

But is it possible that Paul can speak of himself as 'carnal' if he is truly regenerate? For some the use of this term is in itself sufficient proof that Paul is not speaking of believers. But we must note that the term and concept are used in three different senses in Scripture.

1. Unbelievers are essentially carnal

Firstly, 'carnal' sometimes designates those who are unregenerate, who are entirely or exclusively under the control of the flesh. The 'flesh' in this sense denotes man under sin, unregenerate human nature. Such people know nothing of divine grace, or of the Holy Spirit. The sole principle active within them is sin and the flesh. They are therefore said to be carnal. In Romans 7:5 Paul states, 'When we were *in the flesh,* the sinful passions aroused by the law were at work in our bodies, so that we bore fruit for death.' Again in 8:5 he clearly refers to the unbeliever when he declares, 'Those who *live according to the flesh* have their minds set on what the flesh desires, but those who live in accordance with the Spirit have their minds set on what the Spirit desires.' And again in 8:8 he states, 'Those *in the flesh* cannot please God.' It is clear that to be 'in the flesh', to 'live according to the flesh', and to have your mind 'set on what the flesh desires' all mean to be unregenerate, in a state of sin and therefore to know nothing of the gracious sanctifying power of the Holy Spirit in your life.

It is important, however, to notice that here in 7:14 Paul does not say that he is in the flesh, or controlled by the flesh. He is not at all describing a life controlled by his basic sinful human nature, the fallen depraved nature he inherited from Adam, polluted, with a propensity towards evil. Such terms would be wholly misleading. Rather he is honestly confessing the fact that when he considers the perfection and spirituality of God's law, he is conscious of his own many imperfections, and is thus constrained with anguish to confess them. In comparison with the absolute spirituality of God's holy law, he finds no more appropriate term to describe his imperfections than 'carnal'. The relics of sin are still there, and he painfully recognizes that fact.

2. Christians can be carnal in certain respects

The term 'carnal' is also applied by Paul to Christians who, when compared with others, give evidence in some respects of deficiency of spirituality. In 1 Corinthians 3:1 he addresses a specific group of believers whom he designates as 'carnal': 'Brothers, I could not address you as spiritual, but as *carnal [sarkinois]* — mere infants in Christ. I gave you milk, not solid food, for you were not yet ready for it. Indeed you are still not ready. You are still *carnal [sarkikoi]*. For when one says, "I follow Paul", and another, "I follow Apollos", are you not mere men *[anthropoi]*?'

It is clear that Paul's use here of the concept of flesh refers not to the fact that these Corinthians possess human bodies, are part of flesh-and-blood humanity and so are in the flesh. Rather he uses 'flesh' or 'carnal' in a deprecatory, moral sense. There was something in their behaviour that reminded him of the sort of attitude and actions one expects from those who are part of unregenerate humanity, who are still under the dominion of sin and know nothing of grace or the Spirit.

But Paul does not mean to say that their carnality was evidence that those guilty of party strife were not believers. Throughout he has assumed they are regenerate. In chapter 1 he designates them as 'those sanctified in Christ Jesus'; they are recipients of the grace of God and have been enriched by Christ 'in all your speaking and in all your knowledge' (1:2-5). They clearly are children of God. However, when he contrasts them with the state of spiritual maturity which God requires among his people, in certain respects he has to admit they are carnal. There were jealousy, quarrelling and division among them; they were behaving like babes in Christ; they could be fed only on milk. 'Though grace was real and sincere, it was weak: so the flesh remained strong and little subdued in them,' comments Fraser.[2] They were *comparatively* carnal. Their disputes and envyings showed their attainment in the Christian life to be poor. In this limited and comparative sense, then, some Christians may be said to be carnal. But to be called 'carnal' is not necessarily equivalent to being categorized as 'in the flesh', or unregenerate.

Care must be taken not to construct on the basis of this distinction a two-tier system of Christianity, by which Christians are classified as 'spiritual' or 'carnal' in an absolute sense according to their spiritual achievements, and an easy once-for-all step of elevation to the 'higher-life' experience is offered on simplistic terms. Such Perfectionist, or higher-life, theories are unknown to Paul, and seriously undermine the biblical doctrine of regeneration.

The fact that Paul in 1 Corinthians 3 rebukes those whom he has already designated as sanctified in Christ Jesus for behaving in a carnal manner does not mean that he recognizes such a category of Christian. He rebukes them, not for failing to attain to privileges which some Christians attained to, or for failing to pass from a low category of Christians to a higher one. Rather he rebukes them for acting, despite their privileges and standing in Christ, like babes and like the unregenerate, in one area of their lives.

Reisinger sums up the position well when he writes, 'This is very different from saying that the Apostle here recognizes the existence of a distinct group of Christians who can be called "carnal". When Paul comes to speak of classes, he knows only two, as is clear in chapter 2 of this same Epistle [1 Corinthians] where he divides men into "natural" and "spiritual". The spiritual may be but babes in grace and babes in knowledge. Their faith may be weak. Their love may be in early bud, their spiritual senses may be but little exercised, their faults may be many; but if "the root of the matter" is in them and if they have passed from death unto life — passed out of nature into that which is beyond nature — Paul puts them down in another class. They are all spiritual men although in some aspects of their behaviour they may temporarily fail to appear as such.'[3]

3. All Christians are relatively carnal so long as they are on earth

In Romans 7 we find a third use of the concept of carnality. Here Paul compares himself in his regenerate state with the spiritual law of God, and expresses in very strong terms the contrast he discovers. Compared to his former unregenerate self, he is not carnal in the sense he once was, but spiritual. He is not part of unregenerate humanity, a man in the flesh, under the power and dominion of sin. Unregenerate Paul would never have expressed himself as he does here. Nor is he carnal in a way comparable to the weak, immature brethren who 'walked as men', and among whom a specific outcrop of carnality was manifest, as at Corinth. Compared with such people he is spiritual. But when he considers his life in the light of the spiritual law of God, and the strict holiness it demands, he confesses he is carnal.

This humble and honest assessment of himself and his spiritual attainment arises from a change of perspective. His spiritual perspicacity and sensibility have been heightened. He is conscious that he is still in the body of sinful flesh, an imperfect human body, and is subject to all the imperfections in which sin has left him. He is still in an imperfect state and, by reason of that imperfection, is unequal to the demands of laws which are totally spiritual, reflecting the perfection of the Spirit of God. So he expresses his feelings with deep humility.

Paul is here speaking of himself as representative of the Christian, every Christian, and describes the Christian as carnal in the sense that even in him there remains, so long as he continues to live this mortal life, that which is radically opposed to God. In chapter 8, however, he will make it abundantly clear that he does not regard the believer as being carnal in the same unqualified way that the natural man is carnal. There he states, 'What the law was powerless to do in that it was weakened by the flesh, God did by sending his own Son in the likeness of sinful man to be a sin offering. And so he condemned sin in sinful man, in order that the righteous requirements of the law might be fully met in us, who do not live according to the flesh but according to the Spirit... You, however, are controlled not by the flesh but by the Spirit, if the Spirit of God lives in you. And if anyone does not have the Spirit of Christ, he does not belong to Christ' (8:3-4,9).

Hendriksen summarizes the position thus: 'When Romans 7:14 is interpreted in the light of verses 22 to 25, it becomes clear that the one who in verse 14 deplores his sinful condition is the same person who in the chapter's closing verses expresses his delight in the law of God, looks forward with impassioned and irresistible longing to the day of his deliverance from his present momentous inner struggle, and is filled with the blessed assurance that victory is bound to come; in fact in principle it is here already.

'However, for the present the Christian is living in an era in which two ages, the old and the new, overlap. There was a time when Paul was "exclusively a sinner". There will be a time when he will be "exclusively a saint". Right now, as he is dictating this letter, he is "a sinner-saint". A "saint" to be sure; but also still a "sinner"; hence the tension, the inner conflict.'[4]

This tension and frustration, caused by the limitations of the present world-order, are described also in 2 Corinthians 5:1-4. There Paul writes, 'We groan, longing to be clothed with our heavenly dwelling... While we are in this tent, we groan and are burdened.' Clearly he is speaking of something intensely spiritual and internal. Concerning his external behaviour he could write to the Thessalonians in a very different vein: 'You are witnesses and so is God, of how holy, righteous and blameless we were among you who believed' (1 Thess. 2:10). But when conscious of the spirituality of the law, he is bowed down and confesses, 'I am carnal, sold under sin.' This is the language of deep sorrow and mourning over remaining sin which burdens the thoughtful, enlightened believer.

Such expressions are consistent with the confessions of believers throughout the ages. Abraham when viewing the perfection of the divine nature exclaimed, 'I am nothing but dust and ashes' (Gen. 18:27). Jacob made a similar confession when he said, 'I am not worthy of the least of all the mercies ... which you have shown your servant' (Gen. 32:10, NKJV).

The experience of Job is particularly interesting and relevant. When finally the Lord reveals to him something of his transcendent majesty and glory, Job has to confess,

'I have heard of you by the hearing of the ear,
but now my eye sees you.
Therefore I abhor myself
and repent in dust and ashes'

(Job 42:6, NKJV).

The two contrasting experiences of Job, before and after his vision of the Lord, are similar to Paul's contrasting views of himself in Philippians 3:6 and Romans 7:14. In the former he writes of his conceived grounds of confidence as a natural man before God. Then his boast was that, as touching the righteousness which was according to law, that is, external legalistic righteousness, he was blameless. Then he was hearing with the ear only, as Job put it. When he discovered the spirituality of the law, he could only bow his head in shame and confession.

We found similar expressions in John Newton's poem when in answer to his request that he might grow in grace, the Lord crossed all his fair schemes and laid him low, and explained,

These inward trials I employ
From self and pride to set thee free,
And break thy schemes of earthly joy,
That thou mayest seek thy all in me.

This was not a negative and debilitating experience for John Newton. His heart was all the more drawn out after his Lord, and his longings after Christ increased. Let the spirituality of God's law humble us indeed, and awaken us to seek our Saviour all the more strenuously!

Something of the ardour of this insatiable longing after Christ and perfection is described most beautifully in the Song of Solomon, when the Shulamite is brought to the place where she pants after the fulness of the blessing of being with her beloved. But such cloudless fellowship is not perfectly experienced in this life.

Sold as a slave to sin

The second accusation which Paul brings against himself seems an even stronger expression than 'carnal'. It has been compared with what is said in the Old Testament of Ahab, who 'sold himself to do evil in the eyes of the Lord' (1 Kings 21:20,25; cf. 2 Kings 17:17), and some commentators assume the term used here by Paul must have the same force and connotation. If that were so, we should be forced to conclude that the apostle was speaking of an unbeliever, for the reference to Ahab is undoubtedly to one who deliberately abandoned himself to do evil. This, of course, could never be said of a regenerate man. He may have his lapses, be imperfect, disgrace himself and dishonour his Lord, but he never deliberately apostatizes and abandons himself to evil as Ahab did.

It seems probable that the idea of slavery is present here in the term that is used. That in itself is no indication that Paul's slavery to sin partook of the same characteristics as that of Ahab. The experiences of the two men were very different. It is one thing to experience the power of sin in one's life; it is quite another actively to sell oneself to the power of evil.

Clearly there is a difference between, on the one hand, a prisoner of war, who as a result of his capture finds himself a slave to his enemy but longs for his liberty and still considers himself a loyal soldier of his king; and, on the other, a man who deliberately and willingly sells himself as a mercenary into the employment of his enemy. They are in two very different situations and they would express themselves very differently. In the first case the language would be that of complaint; in the second that of compliance.

The description of Ahab in 1 Kings is the calm, objective, balanced record of a historian who passes an inspired judgement on the wicked king. He observes that Ahab's life was so characterized by conscious, deliberate, habitual disobedience to the law of the Lord that it seemed as if he had willingly capitulated to evil, and surrendered all his faculties to perpetrate evil. He had sold himself into the slavery of sin. But when Paul uses the expression of slavery to depict his experience, he does so with great personal sadness and sorrow. He deeply regrets that his heart is not entirely spiritual, that his life is not in perfect accordance with God's law. He feels that he has been unwillingly taken captive by a tyrant who compels him to do things he has no pleasure in doing. The dominant desire of his heart is perfect conformity to the holy law of God, but he sadly has to confess that much is lacking. The captivity to sin of which Paul here speaks is quite contrary to the service and experience to which he is permanently committed, and for which he most ardently longs. Romans chapters 6 and 8 describe his true state and experience. They are the context against which Paul's account of his 'slavery' is to be considered, and there the atmosphere is one of triumph and victory. But the deceitfulness of sin, of which he has just spoken in 7:11, causes him much chagrin, even in his regenerate state.

Once again Paul's confession may be compared to that of Job, Jacob and Abraham who, before fresh revelations of the ineffable being of God, confessed, 'I am vile', 'I am unworthy...' and, 'I am nothing but dust and ashes.' In similar fashion, Paul's confession of servitude is his response to the holiness of God revealed in the law, as the apostle reproaches himself for his transgressions.

Fraser is surely correct when he writes, 'If we overheard a serious upright Christian saying on some occasion, with much regret, "What a slave I am to carnal affections and unruly passions!", we would not regard him unfavourably.' Such a lament would be as entirely consistent with his regenerate state as it was alien to the spirit of Ahab.

Paul's use of the concepts of carnality and slavery, rather than betraying an ungodly and unregenerate state, as some suppose, is in fact evidence of regeneration. Even though, through Christ, Paul has been 'made free from sin', yet so long as his earthly life lasts he still lives under the condition of sin, and is aware of the remaining sin which so distresses him.

'I do not understand [or know] what I do. For what I want to do I do not do, but what I hate I do. And if I do what I do not want to do, I agree that the law is good. As it is, it is no longer I myself who do it, but it is sin living in me' (7:15-17).

Paul's frustrated desire to do good

With verse 15 Paul launches into a long, complex and complicated statement which continues until the end of verse 23. It contains several remarks which at first glance seem confusing. He appears to confess that he does not know what he is doing, and that he is totally frustrated by his inability to do good (7:15). He seems to dissociate himself from any responsibility for his condition, saying it is due to sin living within him (7:17). Further, he confesses that nothing good lives in him, and his desires to do good constantly fail (7:18). He keeps on performing evil (7:19). And once again he attributes his failure to the dominance of sin within him (7:20). It is little wonder that in the light of these statements many commentators have concluded that this cannot possibly reflect Christian experience, and that it must describe the unbeliever's elusive desire for morality, but depressing confession of failure. However, if we work through the passage carefully, paying due attention to the precise phrases Paul uses, we shall see that this is not at all the case.

Verse 15 in the Greek text begins with the conjunction 'therefore'. This links verses 15-23 with verse 14. Having confessed, in the full light of the spirituality of God's law, his unspirituality and 'slavery' to sin, he proceeds to explain more fully what he means by those indictments. He deeply regrets the discrepancy between what he wills and what he achieves. What he did he did not know; what he willed he did not practise.

There is no question here of a psychological dualism, of irrational action on the part of Paul. He is not saying that he was irresponsible for his actions because they were involuntary and totally beyond his control. His action was not irrational. No action is performed without the consent of the will. There is no way in which we can retreat from our actions and attribute them to some force beyond ourselves. 'I do them', declares Paul. There is no suggestion that he is totally unaware of what he is doing, nor that in an absolute sense he is completely and permanently defeated in his desire to do good. Nor does he say that his will is divided — that he wants to do good and at the same time does not want to perform it. His will is united in its direction and desire to perform what is good.

When Paul states, 'I do not know what I do,' he is certainly not denying that his behaviour is that of a conscious agent. The expressions of remorse and regret which follow indicate that he is only too aware of what he is doing. Rather he is explaining that he does not in any way *condone* his behaviour. The verb used here is frequently found in Scripture in the sense of 'to approve', 'to love', 'to delight in', 'to set regard upon' (see for example, Matt. 7:23; Amos 3:2). It is the opposite of 'hate', which occurs in the second part of verse 15, thereby confirming this interpretation. Paul, then, is not denying his understanding of what he is doing, but expressing his frustration and bewilderment at his failure to achieve it. He owns the actions to be fully his, but is ashamed of them.

We must be careful not to tone down Paul's determined will to act, as if it were but a weak desire, a wish, a nostalgic longing. There is no evidence of lack of determined resolution and volition; the problem lies in the fact that this will to perform in practice is ineffective (cf. 7:18-19).

But if Paul truly desires to do what is right, and has to confess his powerlessness to do it, is this not proof that he is speaking of when he was unconverted? How is it possibly compatible with his description of the Christian life in chapter 8? And is not the description of a will to do that has no effect in practice contrary to what Paul says in Philippians: 'God works in you both to will *and to do* for his good pleasure'? (Phil. 2:13, NKJV). There is no mere ineffectual desire there!

In reply, there are several important factors of which we must not lose sight. Firstly, there is no question here of a divided will. Paul constantly asserts that his will is steadfastly directed towards the good. His complaint is that his unified will, entirely directed towards that which is good, does not in fact achieve fully what it desires.

Secondly, Paul does not say that he is never capable of practising the good which he wants to perform. He is speaking in the context of a deeply spiritual understanding of the law of God, and of the absolute perfection of its demands. He is confessing that he does not perform that which is good so constantly and well as he ordinarily desires and wills. His statement in Philippians 2:13 must not be understood as claiming that the believer will always, without exception, desire and perform the good. Such a notion of perfection is foreign to the New Testament (1 John 1:8). Paul's prevailing inclination was towards good, as the following verses make clear, and he is speaking according to the strict spirituality of the law.

Thirdly, Paul docs not condone what he does. This is the source of the conflict throughout the chapter. Paul is not describing the lament of an unregenerate person, nor the frustration of a defeated, carnal Christian. 'He is opening up his heart to his readers concerning the increasing self-discoveries which any advance in the Christian life must necessarily bring. He has been learning the exceeding sinfulness of sin, and the enormity of its hold upon him. Here is the truly Christian experience, but it is that part of it which, through the deceptiveness and shallowness of our hearts, we so rarely come to know. It is quite true, as some have pointed out, that the Holy Spirit is not mentioned by name in this immediate paragraph of the epistle, but his activity is everywhere evident. The situation which the apostle describes is one which is created by the entry of the life of the Spirit into the soul. The more there is of the "Spirit of life in Christ Jesus" in us, the more will the depths of inbred sin be discovered. These are the discoveries of which Paul gives an account here.'[5]

Fourthly, Paul expresses his deep detestation and hatred of sin, which is contrary to the holy, righeous and good law of God. Only those who are regenerate hate sin. Unregenerate men may disapprove of many forms of sin, but their habitually living in it is proof that they love it in many forms, and that in no case do they hate it as sin.

On the basis of what he has just stated in verse 15, that what he desires to do he does not achieve, but what he hates, that in fact he does, Paul draws two deductions concerning his whole position: the first is in verse 16 — he consents that the law is good; the second is in verse 17 — he attributes his dilemma to the presence of indwelling sin.

1. Paul wholeheartedly agrees that the law is good (7:16).

Paul's first deduction is that the logical conclusion of what he has said is that he agrees, or consents, that the law is good. The fact that he regrets his actions, and does not at all approve of them, means that in the fundamental and most characteristic inclinations of his will and heart he agrees with what the law says about them. He consents to the essential goodness of the law. He is in wholehearted agreement with it.

The word 'agree' or 'consent' (AV) is interesting and instructive. It means literally 'to speak with'. Here is someone or something speaking, expressing himself, making a declaration or statement. 'Well', says Paul, 'I speak with it, I am in agreement with it, and consent to it. I do things of which I do not approve. But the law likewise does not approve of them. Well, it is obvious that I am in wholehearted agreement with the law.'

Paul is declaring more than his assent to the law. He is speaking of the object of his will. Already in verse 12 he has declared that the law is holy, and the commandment is holy, righteous and good. In verse 14 he has expressed his conviction that the law is spiritual, and in verse 22 he states that he delights in God's law in his inner being. The whole context therefore argues strongly in favour of the translation 'consent', as expressing the agreement of heart, mind and will.

He consents that the law possesses the highest quality of goodness. It is the transcript of the holy character of God, and indicates the believer's obligation with regard to God's will. Paul discovers that his will consents to it. 'However much he bemoans his condition, there is consolation is his whole-souled endorsement of the law, and of his alignment with it in the most determinative bent of his will.'[6]

We must remember that Paul was not concerned merely to state his own experience, but to prove something concerning the law. He wants firstly to prove that the law is in no way responsible for his failure in practice. He completely exonerates the law of any blame. But ultimately he wants to show that as the law cannot justify the sinner, neither can it sanctify the saint.

Fraser is surely right when he says of this verse, 'This does not fit the prevailing principles of the unregenerate. They can argue in rational theory that the law is good, but not consent with heart and will that it is good, and commands what is good for *me* to do.'

Marcus Rainsford argues similarly: 'Before his conversion Paul discovered the law and the apostle were in antagonism to each other. He was "alive without the law once", and when the law came, its effect on him was to give occasion "to the motions of sin in his members", vivifying and exciting the evil within him to arraign, conflict and slay him. But now his heart *speaks the same thing* as the law. He delights in the law of God after the inner man. He has had a complete and radical change of heart, as in Hebrews 8:10: "I will put my laws in their minds and write them on their hearts."'[7]

Paul is declaring that the fact that there is such conflict within the heart of a Christian proves that there is within him that which acknowledges the goodness and righteousness of the law. This commitment to God's law is, as Paul goes on to say in chapter 8, the work of the Holy Spirit.

2. Paul attributes his dilemma to the influence of indwelling sin (7:17)

Here we find Paul's second deduction derived from his statement in verse 15: 'I do not condone what I do, for what I want to do I do not do, but what I hate I do.' This means that 'I am in agreement with the law which condemns it (7:16). But this being so, it is then not I who do it, but sin that dwells in me' (7:17).

How does he arrive at this deduction? What he has just been saying has raised a problem in his mind. He has confessed that at times he does things that are against the inclination of his heart and the settled direction of his will. He does not condone these actions, and heartily concurs with the law in its condemnation of them. But how then is he to explain the occurrence of sin? The law is not responsible, and he himself detests these actions and does not desire to perform them — yet he does commit them. What then is the explanation? What is responsible? How do they come to occur? His logical deduction and inevitable conclusion are that 'It is then not I who do it, but sin living in me.'

Paul here identifies himself with that determinate will which concurs with the law of God. At the same time he appears to dissociate himself from the sin committed, and from the sin that dwells within him. He places the responsibility for the sin on indwelling sin.

Several important matters should be noted. Firstly, this verse must not be understood as a denial of personal responsibility. Paul is not exonerating himself from blame. His intention is not to deny that he did these things, but to assert that he did them under an influence which is no longer the dominant one in his mind. He is explaining that his violations of divine law were not the true expressions of his new Christian character. In his mind he was 'a slave to God's law' (7:26). This was his true habitual character, though he still occasionally acted under the influence of sin.

John Brown, commenting on this verse, draws attention to other occasions when Paul speaks of a distinction between himself and another agent, without denying personal responsibility. 'When Paul, speaking of his apostolic labours, says, "Not I, but the grace of God that was with me" (1 Cor. 15:10), he does not mean to say that he did not perform these labours, but that he performed them under the influence of the grace of God. Similarly in Galatians 2:20, "I live, yet not I, but Christ liveth in me", he means merely that to Christ he was indebted for the origin and maintenance of his new and better life.'[8]

Secondly, the clear implication of this statement is that Paul is speaking as a Christian. What caused his trouble was not his renewed heart, which approved the law of God, but sin, which continued to dwell within him and of which he was an unwilling slave. He does not minimize the power and extent of indwelling sin, which is beyond his own power and the power of the law to eradicate or control effectively. Nor does he deny his accountability. But he does so with genuine self-condemnation and penitence.

Fraser remarks, 'What here would strike any man free of bias is that this "I" on the side of holiness against sin is the most prevailing and what represents the true character of the man; and that "sin" which he distinguishes from this "I" is not the prevailing reigning power in the man here represented as it is in every unregenerated man.'[9] On this verse Calvin remarks, 'This passage clearly proves Paul is disputing concerning none but the pious who are now regenerated.'[10] Haldane writes, 'No man can disclaim sin, as in this verse it is disclaimed, except the converted man; for who besides can conscientiously and intelligently affirm, "Now it is no more I who do it, but sin that dwelleth in me"?'[11]

Paul's object in this verse is to show that the experience spoken of in verse 15 is consistent with his being a Christian. Charles Hodge paraphrases these verses thus: 'If it is true that I really approve and love the law, and desire to be conformed to it, I am no longer the willing slave of sin; to the depth and power of original sin is to be attributed the fact that I am not entirely delivered from its influence.' He perceptively concludes, 'This is obviously connected with the main object of the main passage. For if sin remains and exerts its power, not withstanding our disapprobation, and in despite of all our efforts, it is clear that we must look for deliverance to something out of ourselves, and that the mere perceptive power of the law cannot remove the evil.'[12]

Thirdly, this verse explains the dualism which is the cause of the conflict which runs through the chapter. As we have seen, there is a dualism here, but it is a dualism belonging not to the Christian's will, but to his double situation. He does not desire the good and the evil at the same time. Throughout the passage his will is solely directed towards the good. The duality is caused by the presence of an extraneous power within him besides his own ego, the sin dwelling in him. This verse is an acknowledgement of the extent to which sin dwelling in the Christian exercises an enervating influence in his life. This is the result of the Christian's double position. He is 'in Christ', but so long as he dwells on earth he is still in sinful flesh (7:18), hence the tension and conflict. 'In the Spirit' he delights in God's will; but still the flesh exercises its effect, with the result that the will is not carried out to corresponding performance. In Christ he belongs to the new age, the dominion of life; but he still finds himself in the midst of the present age. The tension, or dualism, is not that of a divided and discordant soul, but of the Christian's double situation in two ages.

Fourthly, Paul is careful to state that sin 'lives' or 'dwells', in him, whereas before, when he was unregenerate, sin 'reigned' in death. Sin, exceedingly sinful, subtle, insidious, threatening and enervating sin, still dwells in him, but it does not reign. It will never again have dominion over the life of the believer, for 'Grace [reigns] through righteousness unto eternal life' (5:21, NKJV). 'Sin shall not have dominion over you, for you are not under law but under grace' (6:14, NKJV). 'Count yourselves dead to sin [to its rule, reign and dominion] but alive to God in Christ Jesus' (6:11).

Sin dwelling in the apostle is just another name for the measure of ignorance, error and worldly propensity which, despite the change which had taken place in Paul's life, still remained. The sin-power which once entirely possessed and controlled him has not yet been expelled. It still maintains itself in him, and lurks in his members. It is a question now of habitation, not of domination. In the believer there now dwells another power, the Holy Spirit ('The Spirit of God dwells in you,' 8:9, NKJV). He too has taken up residence in the believing heart, but in contrast to the defeated power, sin, which lurks in the dark corners of the believer's heart in the form of the relics in sin, waiting to be dislodged totally and permanently, the Spirit rules, reigns and dominates to the extent that Paul can say that believers 'do not live according to the sinful nature but according to the Spirit' (8:4).

'I know that nothing good lives in me, that is, in my flesh. For I have the desire to do what is good, but I cannot carry it out' (7:18).

In this verse Paul expands on the statement he made in verse 17 that sin dwells in him. Not only must he confess the humbling fact of indwelling sin, but also the powerlessness of self to perform the good. 'I know that nothing good lives [or dwells] in me.'

But can this frank admission possibly be true of a renewed man? Was he not born of God? Had he not received the Holy Spirit? Had he not been married to him who was raised from the dead in order that he might bear fruit unto God? (7:4). Even as he writes, Paul is conscious that in its full sense the statement he makes concerning the absence of good within him could not be true of him as a regenerate man. He hastens therefore to add the qualifying clause, 'that is, in my flesh'. Paul, fully conscious of the duality of his double standing, has distinguished in verse 17 'no longer I myself' from 'sin dwelling in me'; now he distinguishes 'in me' from 'in my flesh'.

This distinction implies that there is more to be said about the man being spoken of than that he is flesh. This indicates that Paul is speaking of himself as a Christian. Lenski comments, 'We should not suppose that sin dwells in him in the sense of having possession of the whole. The sin-power is "in him" indeed, but only "in his flesh", which certainly does not mean only in the physical body, but in the old sinful nature that is left in the regenerate. It has been well said that no unregenerate man could thus speak of his flesh, for such a man is all flesh and not merely so in parts. The flesh still left in us is wholly bad and thus affords a place for the sin-power to dwell.'[13]

Throughout this passage Paul is opening up his heart to his readers concerning the increasing self-discoveries which any advance in the Christian life must necessarily bring. He has been learning the exceeding sinfulness of sin, and the enormity of its hold upon him. Commenting on this conflict, Kevan writes, 'Here is the truly Christian experience; but it is that part of which, through the deceptiveness and shallowness of our hearts, we so rarely come to know. It is quite true, as some have pointed out, that the Holy Spirit is not mentioned by name in this immediate paragraph of the epistle, but his activity is everywhere evident. The situation which the apostle describes is one which is created by the entry of the life of the Spirit into the soul. The more there is of "the Spirit of life in Christ Jesus" in us, the more will the depths of inbred sin be discovered. These are the discoveries of which Paul gives an account here.'[14]

When Paul comes in verse 25 to summarize the contents of this passage, he identifies two spiritual antagonists which are rival claimants for the loyalty of the will of the believer, and two distinct areas of operation: 'I myself in my mind am a slave to God's law, but in the flesh [I am] a slave to the law of sin.' God's holy law on the one hand, and sin on the other — these are the rival claimants in this Spirit-provoked conflict. The one has its stronghold, or sphere of operation, in the mind; the other in the flesh. It is his slavery to the law of sin in the flesh which is referred to in verse 18.

Flesh and the believer

The term 'flesh' in Scripture is used to denote different things, its precise meaning varying according to its context.

Firstly, it can denote a physical body, or part of a physical body, whether human or animal (Gen. 40:19; Job 10:11).

Secondly, it can designate mankind in his frailty and creatureliness before God. The emphasis here is on man's weakness, transitoriness and dependence upon the almighty Creator (Isa. 40:6-8; Jer 17:5). There is no absolute body/spirit dualism in Scripture, as though matter were inherently evil and spirit alone good. Man is a being of flesh, and possesses the appropriate appetites. These natural appetites are legitimate in themselves, and the faithful Creator has provided for their satisfaction.

Thirdly, flesh is also used to describe fallen mankind, deprived of the Spirit of God, dominated by sinful appetites and depraved instincts. This is the whole unregenerated and unsanctified nature of mankind. In this moral sense flesh stands for the force, or principle, of indwelling sin in fallen human nature. We find passages in Paul's writings where 'the flesh' is totally identified with what is sinful (Gal. 5:13-25; Rom. 13:14; 1 Cor. 3:1; Gal. 6:8; Eph. 2:3,11; Col. 2:18,23).

'Flesh' in this sense signifies autonomous man, in sinful revolt against his Creator, manifesting his rebellion through his bodily faculties and members, both physical and mental, or spiritual. It denotes the whole personality of man as organized in the wrong direction, towards sinful pursuits rather than the service of God. It has its 'lusts' and 'desires' (Eph. 2:3). 'The carnal mind [the mind of the flesh] is enmity against God; for it is not subject to the law of God, nor indeed can be' (Rom. 8:7, NKJV). The man whose horizon is limited by the flesh is by that fact opposed to God. He lives 'according to the flesh' (Rom. 8:13), that flesh which 'lusts against the Spirit' (Gal. 5:17, NKJV). For a dreadful list of the works of the flesh we need only consult Galatians 5:19-21. What a fearful catalogue this is, comprising grossly physical sins, but also subtle vices that belong to man as a spiritual being!

Flesh contemplated in this aspect is man's sinful nature, that aspect, or created structure, of man's nature in which sin manifests itself. It is the force or principle of indwelling sin in fallen human nature, man apart from the influence of the Holy Spirit.

Finally, flesh is used in connection with the remnants of sin in the life of the believer to denote the sinful nature which is still associated with him.

Flesh as physical body is not itself in essence sinful. It is possible to live a life of faith in the flesh. Paul clearly testifies to this in Galatians 2:20 when he writes, 'I have been crucified with Christ and I no longer live, but Christ lives in me. The life I live in the body [lit., the flesh] I live by faith in the Son of God, who loved me and gave himself for me.' Again in 2 Corinthians 5:9 he says, 'We make it our goal to please him, whether we are at home in the body or away from it.' Christ himself lived in a physical body without committing sin.

Nevertheless, because of 'the weakness of the flesh', an association exists between life in the flesh and sin (Rom. 7:5,8; 8:8; 2 Cor. 7:1). Thus 'flesh' becomes synonymous with the sinful nature of fallen man, which in the case of the believer opposes his higher self, with its Spirit-provoked aspirations. This virtual identification of flesh with sin is particularly striking in Romans 7, where flesh appears so passive and is dominated by an active personal power called sin. Since sin is expressed through our bodily members, it is symbolically described as flesh. But just as our bodily functions include not just physical desires and appetites but the activity of the higher faculties of mind, heart and emotions, so flesh is responsible for sins of mind and heart as well as more obviously physical sins. Flesh, then, is that aspect of man's nature which gives sin its opportunity, even within the life of the believer.

Flesh and the present age

There exists a close relationship between flesh and the present age or world-order. This relationship is reflected in Paul's statements in Romans 7.

Paul consistently speaks of two 'ages' or world-orders. In Ephesians 1 he states that Christ has been exalted 'far above all rule and authority, power and dominion, and every title that can be given, not only in the *present age* but also in the *one to come*' (v.21). Elsewhere he may speak only of this age or world — 'Do not conform to the pattern of *this world*' (Rom. 12:2). 'Where is the philosopher of *this age*?' (1 Cor. 1:20); 'The god of *this age*…' (2 Cor. 4:4); '… to rescue us from *the present evil age*' (Gal. 1:4) — but the implication is that there is another age to come. This age is that of the flesh, while the age to come is that of the Spirit.

It is clear, then, that for Paul 'the flesh', the sphere of sinful man, represents a state of existence far greater than the individual. It is cosmic in scope. Sin and flesh are the epitome of the old age, while the Spirit is the pervading power of the new. Those whose lives are characterized by having their minds set on the flesh (Rom. 8:7), and of whom it can be said that they are 'in the flesh' (Rom. 7:5), are entirely bound to the present world-order, and know nothing of grace or the liberating power of the Spirit (Rom. 8:3).

How is it possible, then, for Paul to speak of a regenerate person as being affected, or hampered, by the flesh? Has he not been rescued from the old dominion of flesh, sin and death, and delivered into the sphere of Spirit, holiness and life? The relevance of the question is seen in the exposition of John Murray, who maintains that the following propositions are clearly implied in what Paul says in Romans 7:18.

1. The flesh is wholly sinful — no good dwells in it.

2. The flesh is still associated with his person — the flesh is *his* flesh, and is *in him.*

3. Sin is also associated with his person, for it is in his flesh that sin adheres.[15]

This being so, how can Paul possibly have in mind the experience of a believer? The answer is to be found in the believer's dual status as living in two worlds, ages, or world-orders at the same time. So long as he lives upon this earth, the believer must live 'in the flesh', and is thus in the 'body of death' (7:24), that is, in a mortal body, a physical body and a mode of earthly existence under the sentence of death, and destined to pass away. In Christ he has been liberated from the law of sin and death (8:2) and no longer lives according to the flesh (8:4). The tension he experiences is due to the fact that at one and the same time he is a participant in the new age, while, at the same time, he is in some way in the old.

Galatians 5:13-26 throws much light on the conflict described in Romans 7. There Paul speaks of sin in the believer, and uses the concept of 'flesh' to portray it. 'For the flesh desires what is contrary to the Spirit, and the Spirit what is contrary to the flesh. They are in conflict with each other, so that you do not do what you want' (5:17). Flesh is a real power contending for dominion over the life of a man, and set in deadly opposition to the Spirit of God. But despite the intensity and constancy of the struggle, these verses emphasize the triumph of the Spirit. 'Live by the Spirit, and you will not gratify the desires of the flesh' (5:16); 'If we live in the Spirit, let us also walk in the Spirit' (5:25, NKJV). This victory is echoed in Romans 7:25 and Romans 8.

Behind this conflict which rages in the life of the believer lies the cosmic warfare between God and Satan, light and darkness, and the historic redemptive triumph of Christ on the cross. This triumph has relevance to every believer, and must be worked out in his or her personal life. The new age has burst upon him. 'Those who belong to Christ Jesus have crucified the flesh with its passions and desires' (Gal. 5:24). This is a plain statement of fact, as clear as those Paul makes when he writes: 'We died to sin... We know that our old self was crucified with him...' (Rom. 6:2, 6); and 'You are not in the flesh but in the Spirit' (Rom. 8:9, NKJV). The great eschatological-redemptive historical event assures our participation in the victory of the new age of grace. But the indicative of redemption carries with it the impelling imperative: 'Since we live by the Spirit, let us walk by the Spirit!' Walking by, or in, the Spirit is the real subject of the passage. If in our day-to-day realization of salvation we discover that the flesh still afflicts us, this is due to our double standing within the two worlds or ages. Our citizenship is in heaven, and yet we find ourselves still living in the body, in this present evil age.

The parallels between Galatians 5 and Romans 7 are so obvious as to confirm us in our understanding of Romans 7 as having reference to conflict within the heart of the believer. There can be no shadow of doubt that Galatians 5 is descriptive of the experience of a truly regenerate person. The same conflict and the same victory are echoed in Romans 7.

This conflict which goes on in the heart of the believer is just another aspect of the cosmic conflict between the forces of light and the forces of darkness, between 'this present evil age' and 'the age to come', which has already dawned in our hearts by the Holy Spirit of God. 'Spirit' in the Galatians passage is not the spirit of man, nor the new nature, but the Spirit of God. This fact is explicit in Galatians; in Romans 7:14-25 it is implicit, but it becomes explicit from 8:4 onwards.

If we feel within ourselves conflict and tension between a sincere desire to do God's will and at the same time a downward pull to follow our sinful impulses, it is because two worlds are in conflict. There is tension between what has 'already' been accomplished and that which has 'not yet' been fully implemented. The great eschatological intervention of God in Christ has 'already' taken place, but the consummation has 'not yet' come. History is moving inexorably towards the completion of redemption, but until then the tension found in chapter 7, and reflected also in 8:23, remains true. 'We ourselves ... groan inwardly as we wait eagerly for our adoption as sons, the redemption of our bodies.' And this groaning has cosmic dimensions: 'We know that the whole creation has been groaning as in the pains of childbirth right up to the present time' (8:22). 'The creation itself will be liberated from its bondage to decay and brought into the glorious freedom of the children of God' (8:21).

Nygren has made a valuable contribution to our understanding of this passage by describing the tension, or dualism, as not that of a 'divided and discordant soul', but of the Christian's 'double situation due to his position in the two aeons',[16] belonging to the new aeon, or age, through Christ, yet living in the flesh. Yet we must take to heart Murray's warning that besides the understanding of sin as power, and freedom from sin as the new status secured for the believer in Christ, there is much that is intensely personal and ethical in the second half of verse 18, and in verse 19.[17]

Personal human experience is very much to the fore in these verses. The struggle is very real in the life of the believer. As the flesh dogs his steps, so sin saddens and grieves him. Similarly the triumphs assured us in this passage and in Galatians 5 are personal and individual. The active responsibility of the believer in the struggle is enlisted. We are to 'walk in the Spirit' in order not to 'fulfil the desires of the flesh'. The Spirit does not short-circuit human faculties. As Ridderbos remarks, 'The principle of the Spirit does not make human effort unnecessary, but arouses it and equips it to put all its forces into the services of the Spirit.'[18] Another aspect of the struggle is that it is continuous, and no one can claim complete victory in this life. 'Paul therefore declares that believers, so long as they are in this life, whatever may be the earnestness of their endeavours, do not obtain such a measure of success as to serve God in a perfect manner.'[19]

The inward and personal nature of the struggle is very real for the believer. He feels the intensity of the conflict between the power of God and the power of sin within him. He is no mere idle spectator at the fight. Basic to his knowledge that nothing good lives in him, that is, in his flesh, is the fact that while he can desire to do good, he is unable to carry out the good he wants to do (7:18). By these words we should, with Calvin, understand Paul to mean, not that the

Christian has absolutely nothing beyond an ineffectual desire, but that what he does never fully corresponds to his will. Sometimes he may fail to carry it out at all; sometimes he may even do the very opposite of what he wants to do; but even his best actions, in which he comes nearest to accomplishing the good he desires, are always stained and spoiled by his egotism.

'For what I do is not the good I want to do; no, the evil I do not want to do — this I keep on doing. Now if I do what I do not want to do, it is no longer I who do it, but it is sin living in me that does it' (7:19-20).

These verses are virtually a repetition of what has been said in verses 15-17. Paul defines the thing willed but not performed as the 'good', and the thing not willed but practised as the 'evil'. Further, he explains his conclusion that responsibility for the evil that he commits must be attributed to sin living in him rather than to himself. He is not, of course, asserting his own innocence or denying his own complicity in sin. No sin is involuntary, and Paul well knows it. Rather he is establishing that such sins are not the characteristic and wilful expressions of the man he is in Christ. Hodge expresses this well when he paraphrases the meaning as follows: 'The things which I do, when contrary to the characteristic desires and purposes of my heart, are to be considered as the acts of a slave. They are indeed my own acts, but not being performed with the full and joyful purpose of the heart, are not to be regarded as a fair criterion of character.'[20]

Perhaps a similar situation could be envisaged where a citizen of a country overrun by the enemy looks back with deep regret on actions he performed under the compulsion of an evil alien invading force. His actions were evil, despicable and inexcusable, but they were performed in the context of warfare and illegitimate enemy occupation, and were not representative of the person he knows himself to be. This does not exonerate him from blame, but it does explain how it came about that he performed such evil actions, so totally inconsistent with his desires and intentions and the normal bent of his life.

'So I find this law at work: When I want to do good, evil is right there with me. For in my inner being I delight in God's law; but I see another law at work in the members of my body, making war against the law of my mind and making me a prisoner of the law of sin at work within my members' (7:21-23).

In the closing verse of the chapter Paul concludes his argument that the law is not in itself responsible for the evil state of mankind. He does so by drawing attention to what he himself discovers his experience to be. He is recapitulating, and summarizes the situation he has described in the preceding verses.

We note three matters of particular interest.

Firstly, the expressions are particularly *personal*. Paul is not dealing with mere conjecture or abstract theory. He has personal experience of strife and tension within his own heart as he longs to please God. How easy it is for us to discuss glibly the things of God, and theoretically to define spiritual warfare or a doctrine of sanctification! Let us become aware of what is happening in our hearts, with a view to progressing in the pathway of holiness!

Secondly, he discovers *two laws* which are at work in his members: God's law and the law of sin. These two mutually incompatible laws wage warfare within him, and are spiritual antagonists. This is the explanation of our experience, the description of the state of the believer's heart. There can be no quietism in our souls so long as this state of affairs lasts. Not ease but vigilance must be the Christian's constant attitude.

Thirdly, these two laws exercise their influence in *two different areas*: the law of God in the 'inner being' (7:22), as the law of the mind (7:23); and the law of sin within the members of his body (7:23).

Paul begins the paragraph by declaring that he finds a principle operative in his life. When he wants to do good, evil is right there with him (7:21). The evil propensity of his nature (which he later defines as the 'law of sin' at work within his members, 7:23,25), is present as a rule or principle of action frustrating him in his desire to do good.

In verse 22 he proceeds to explain that antithesis. If we ask how it is possible that when there is a determinate will to do good, evil can be present, the answer is that there are two rival and antithetical laws which affect us, the law of God and the law of sin. This is stated clearly in verses 22 and 23.

Here we have the two spiritual antagonists, both claimants for the loyalty of his will. One is sin, and the other is the holy law of God. Here are the irreconcilable foes in the Spirit-provoked battle for man. The battlefield is Paul himself. He is clearly distinguished from the rival forces, though he is the one in whose life the strife rages. By his use of the pronouns 'I' and 'me', he distinguishes himself from the contestants. Nevertheless he is an active person who has yet to identify himself with one side or the other. He is the battlefield, but the battlefield is a living person. He cannot remain detached from the powers that fight for supremacy within his life. When he was unregenerate he was completely 'in the flesh', and on the side of sin. Now that he is a child of God, he allies himself with 'the mind', and desires to fulfil the law of God. The battle scene is presented very clearly in verse 25, where all five elements are spoken of: 'So then, *I myself* in *my mind* am a slave to *God's law*, but in *the flesh* a slave to *the law of sin*'

There is no split personality represented here. There is only one 'self', or centre of consciousness, in the believer. The 'old man' and the 'new man' represent not two persons, but two principles of behaviour or mind-sets in which the self at some time or other allows itself to be directed. For Paul, as Kevan puts it, 'The old way has been definitely "put off", and the new has been "put on": he is now altogether and only on the side of the new' (Rom. 6:6). He will declare this fact in verse 25 when, after having surveyed the awful battle scene and described the intensity of the conflict, he thanks God for the assurance of final victory 'through Jesus Christ our Lord'. He then reminds us of his true allegiance to the principle of righteousness: 'I myself in my mind am a slave to God's law.' Kevan continues, 'Paul's true self, his regenerate self, his new self, his Spirit-indwelt self, comes down on the side of the holy law of God.'[21]

In verse 22 we have the first half of the antithesis: 'In my inner being I delight in God's law. This is a clear indication that the person represented in this passage is regenerate. He delights in God's law, and he does so not superficially, but in his inner being.

Paul declares his positive *delight in the law of God*. Having expressed his recognition of the holiness, justice and goodness of the law (7:12,16), and having declared its spirituality (7:14), he strongly asserts that he himself has personal delight in it. 'What the law requires and recommends to me, I take delight in,' says the apostle.

Now nothing is more characteristic of a believer than his delight in God's law. He loves it as the revelation of God's good and perfect will, and embraces it with gladness. He delights in the holiness, justice, goodness and spirituality of its demands. Thus the psalmist declares, 'I delight in your commands because I love them' (Ps. 119:47); 'Direct me in the path of your commands, for there I find delight' (Ps. 119:35). In the Scriptures, delighting in the law of God is presented as a mark of a regenerate person. Indeed this is what distinguishes the righteous from the wicked (Ps. 1:2).

But is there no sense in which unbelievers may take pleasure in God's law? Certainly in Christ's parable of the sower, what was sown on rocky places represents the unconverted man who hears the word and at once receives it with joy, but fails to produce fruit (Matt. 13:5-6,20-21). Similarly, Herod liked to listen to John the Baptist, without apparently any response of faith in his message (Mark 6:20), and the unbelieving Jews listened to Christ with delight (Mark 12:37).

Such statements would seem to undermine the absolute distinction between the attitude of the righteous to God's law and that of the wicked, as represented in Psalm 119. Yet there are important differences between the two situations. The verses we have just quoted from the Gospels do not speak of the law, but of the gospel. It is one thing for a man to take pleasure in hearing good news of remission of sins, deliverance from wrath and eternal happiness, and quite another to take delight in the law of God. Paul's complaint in Romans 2:18-24 is that the unconverted Jews delighted to know God's holy ways, but they clearly did not delight in the law of God.

Paul clarifies the position more fully, and makes it abundantly plain that it is the delight of the believer that he has in mind, by adding the significant qualifying phrase, 'in my inner being', or 'according to the inner man'. This phrase has been variously translated as, 'In so far as the inner man is concerned', or, 'I, in so far as I am that inner man'. It is no superficial delight that he has in mind. It is in the depths of his moral and spiritual being, and that as a renewed man, that he delights in God's law.

Those who deny that this whole section of Romans refers to the believer interpret the phrase 'the inner being', or 'the inner man', in a psychological sense as referring to the higher part of man, his faculty or reason, or the mind. They find the key to the understanding of the phrase in a metaphysical distinction between body and spirit, mind and matter (so Godet, Leenhardt, Sanday and Headlam). They find support for this distinction in the contrast Paul makes in verse 25 between 'the mind' and 'the flesh'. But there Paul is not contrasting mind and body, but mind and flesh, as a moral principle. Throughout this whole section Paul is speaking ethically. There is no question here of a metaphysical distinction between body and spirit, mind and matter. He has been contrasting the good he wanted to do with the evil that he did not want, and analysing his conduct in the light of ethical criteria. He declares that the determinate will to do the good is representative of his deepest and truest self, or the inward man. Despite all the frustration of his will in its determination to do the good, it remains true that he delights in the law of God. 'And this delight is not peripheral but belongs to that which is deepest and inmost in his moral and spiritual being.'[22]

Paul's use of the concept of the 'inner man' elsewhere in his writings confirms this interpretation of the phrase here. In all his letters he never uses the phrase except with reference to the regenerate. Further, virtually identical expressions are found in two passages, where they are undoubtedly applied to the regenerate, to the 'new man', the soul of man renewed by the Holy Spirit, and to him alone.

In 2 Corinthians 4:16 Paul writes, 'Therefore we do not lose heart. Even though our outward man is perishing, yet the inward man is being renewed day by day' (NKJV). The phrase 'the inward man' cannot here refer to man's mind or rational faculty, for his rational faculties diminish as he declines in body and natural faculties. The principle of grace, sanctification and glorification, however, is maintained and renewed in the new man, the inner, regenerate man.

The other occasion where this phrase, 'the inner man', is found is Ephesians 3:16. There Paul expresses his prayer for the Ephesian church that God the Father might strengthen them 'with might through his Spirit in the inner man', so that Christ might dwell in their hearts by faith, and that they might be rooted and grounded in love, and, in common with all the saints, might grasp something of the limitless love of Christ, and be filled with all the fulness of God.

Once again the phrase 'the inner man' is applied to Christians, and particularly to the inner divine life which is daily renewed or strengthened by the ministry of the Spirit.

These passages confirm us in our understanding that Paul in Romans 7:22 is speaking of the believer's delight in the law of the Lord, precisely as in Psalm 119 and elsewhere.

'But I see another law at work in the members of my body, waging war against the law of my mind and making me a prisoner of the law of sin at work within my members' (7:23).

This verse presents the second half of the antithesis begun in verse 22. If in Paul's inner regenerate being he delights in God's law, there is another very different law, the law of sin, warring within his members. Here we are at the very heart of the believer's struggle. Here is set before us the inner conflict which will elicit Paul's painful cry, 'What a wretched man I am!'

The antithesis is between the holy law of God on the one hand, and the wretched 'law' of sin on the other, between delight in God's law in Paul's inner man, and the enervating, captivating 'law' of sin at work in the members of his body.

Clearly in speaking of the 'law of sin' Paul uses the word 'law' metaphorically to denote the exercise of sin's power, authority or control over us. The law of sin is the captivating influence deriving from, and exercised by, sin in the life of the believer. The use of the word 'law' 'is a forceful way of making the point that the power which sin has over us is a terrible travesty, a grotesque parody of that authority over us which belongs by right to God's holy law. Sin's exercising such authority over us is a hideous usurpation of the prerogative of God's law.' [23]

Elsewhere Paul also uses the word 'law' in a figurative sense, speaking of the 'law of faith' (3:27) and the 'law of the Spirit' (8:2). Similarly here he uses the term to express the fact that sin is a powerful principle which can so exercise a tyrannical influence in a believer's life that he is constrained to behave in a way inconsistent with his standing in grace.

This law of sin at work in Paul's members is opposed to the law of God in which he delights in his mind, that is, in his inner being, as he has expressed it in the previous verse. While the law of God regulates his mind, the law of sin is in his members. It is not the law 'of' his members, as if it were the object of their entire service and devotion. It is 'in' the members only as an extraneous usurping power which seeks to draw them away from their consistent legitimate service to God's law. 'Conversion threw the law of sin out of my mind and left this law only in the territory of my members.'[24]

This is the nature of the struggle going on in the life of the believer. On the one hand stands his new spiritual nature, his 'inward man', or his 'mind', which inclines him to delight in the law of God. But on the other stands his old carnal nature, his members, and these two are at war.

The military metaphor is expressed in Paul's confession that he is brought 'into captivity under the law of sin', or made 'a prisoner of the law of sin'. This is a strong statement, similar to that in verse 14, 'sold as a slave to sin', expressing the subjugation of the apostle's will to an influence other than his deepest and most characteristic will. The strength of the expression shows the extent to which Paul finds the position grievous and intolerable. But in the light of what he has said concerning his characteristic spirituality, it must not be read as implying ineffectual striving and total bondage to sin. The conflict is real, intense and deeply felt, but such spiritual conflict is the experience of every Christian, as passages such as Ephesians 6:14-18 and Galatians 5:17-18 show.

Hodge argues strongly in favour of the view adopted in this book when he writes, 'The decision of the question as to what is here meant by "the inward man" depends on what is elsewhere taught in the Scripture concerning the natural state of man. If men, since the fall, are only partially depraved, if sin affects only our lower faculties, leaving the reason undisturbed in its original purity, then by "the inward man" we must understand our rational, as opposed to our sensuous nature. But if the Bible teaches that the whole of man is defiled by sin, and that the principle of spiritual life is something supernatural, then it follows that the conflict here depicted is not that between sense and reason, but that between the new and the old man, the soul as renewed and indwelling sin.'[25]

The extent of spiritual conflict, provoked by the Holy Spirit and experienced by the believer, is well captured by the hymn-writer in the following verses:

Show me myself, O holy Lord;
Help me to look within;
I will not turn me from the sight
Of all my sin.

Just as it is in thy pure eyes
Would I behold my heart;
Bring every hidden spot to light,
Nor shrink the smart.

Not mine, the purity of heart
That shall at last see God;
Not mine, the following in the steps
The Saviour trod.

Not mine, the life I thought to live
When first I took his name:
Mine but the right to weep and grieve
Over my shame.

Yet, Lord, I thank thee for the sight
Thou hast vouchsafed to me;
And, humbled to the dust, I shrink
Closer to thee.

And if thy love will not disown
So frail a heart as mine,
Chasten and cleanse it as thou wilt,
But keep it thine!

'What a wretched man I am! Who will rescue me from this body of death? Thanks be to God — through Jesus Christ our Lord! So then, I myself in my mind am a slave to God's law, but in the sinful nature a slave to the law of sin' (7:24-25).

With this concluding paragraph Paul arrives at the climax of his argument of chapter 7. He depicts in poignant terms the conflict which rages within the heart of someone compelled to live in two worlds at the same time, this present evil age, and the age to come.

'What a wretched man I am!'

This is not a cry of despair, but one of distress. There is a whole world of difference between the two. He is distressed because of the intensity of the conflict he has just described. He feels it keenly, and grieves deeply as he contemplates his imperfections.

The language used here by the apostle is strong, so strong indeed that some have concluded that it cannot possibly apply to a Christian, for he is by definition blessed, not miserable. However, this is a superficial conclusion. While the general tone and characteristic of a believer throughout his life is one of blessedness and joy in many respects, he will nevertheless grieve deeply over the residue of sin within his heart. He does not take remaining sin lightly. Only if the discernment and sensitivity shown by the apostle are absent can the wail of anguish not be understood. And surely such sensitivity should be the experience of every regenerate person.

Throughout this whole section, Paul has not been expressing an apprehension of wrath for unpardoned sin. That has not been the subject in question at all. He has been taking into account the indwelling corruption of a believing heart, and expressing self-loathing for what he finds. The language of verse 24 is suitable only to describe the experience of the regenerate. An unbeliever is indeed wretched and has every reason to give a cry of despair because of the hopelessness of his condition. He may indeed be miserable and filled with anxious fears and deep forebodings. But here we find something quite different: Paul is wretched because he has discovered the awfulness of the principle of sin within his members. That deep spirituality is lacking in the unregenerate.

The distress is expressed in personal terms because, as we have seen, Paul throughout this section is speaking of his own experience. This is no theatrical outcry, nor the reinterpretation of his earlier dilemma, before his conversion, through regenerate eyes. The terms are startlingly personal and poignant. As the apostle writes the words, he feels keenly the wretchedness of his experience of remaining imperfection.

Cranfield is surely right when he writes, 'Inability to recognize the distress reflected in this cry as characteristic of Christian existence argues a failure to grasp the full seriousness of the Christian's obligation to express his gratitude to God by obedience of life... The assertion that this cry could only come from an unconverted heart, and that the apostle must be expressing not what he feels as he writes but the vividly remembered experience of the unconverted man is, we believe, totally untrue. To make it is to indicate ... that one has not considered how absolute are the claims of the grace of God in Jesus Christ. The man whose cry this is is one who, knowing himself to be righteous by faith, desires from the depths of his being to respond to the claims which the gospel makes upon him (cf. v.22). It is the very clarity of his understanding of the gospel and the very sincerity of his love to God, which makes his pain at this continuing sinfulness so sharp.'[26]

'Wretched!' The term used by Paul to express his grief and pain is entirely compatible with an expression of distress, affliction and suffering without in any way implying hopelessness. The burden of indwelling sin was a load which the apostle could neither cast off nor bear. He could only groan under its pressure, and long for a power greater than his.

Clearly the true people of God are distinguished as much by their sorrows and complaints because of remaining corruption as by their joys because of their standing in grace. So long as sin remains within our members, we are not free from hurt. Confessions similar to that of Paul here are found elsewhere in Scripture, on the lips of eminently godly men. As we have already seen, Abraham, pleading before the Lord on behalf of Sodom, declares, 'I am nothing but dust and ashes' (Gen. 18:27). Job too, a blameless and upright man who feared God and shunned evil (Job 1:1,8; 2:3), before the presence of the Almighty cries out, 'Behold I am vile!' 'I abhor myself' (Job 40:4; 42:6, NKJV). Similarly David confesses, 'I am feeble and severely broken; I groan because of the turmoil of the my heart' (Ps. 38:8, NKJV). 'For in you, O Lord, I hope. You will hear, O Lord my God,' and calls the Lord 'my salvation' (Ps. 38:15,22, NKJV). In a similar way Isaiah writes, 'All our righteousnesses are like filthy rags... You are our Father; we are the clay' (Isa. 64:6,8, NKJV).

'Who will deliver me?'

This question, wrung from the heart of the apostle, retains the figure of warfare begun in verse 23. Sin was waging war against the law of Paul's mind, and was making him a prisoner. He therefore asks,

'Who will deliver me?' He longs for someone to liberate him. His question is not so much a request anticipating a response, but a complaint, a cry of distress. It is not the language of ignorance or doubt, but an expression of the depth of his sense of need, and the impossibility of finding deliverance from any source other than the one he immediately identifies — Jesus Christ our Lord.

It is of the greatest importance that we note the nature of the deliverance after which Paul aspires. He desires deliverance 'out of [*ek*] the body of this death', or 'out of this body of death'. Grammatically either translation is possible, but in either case the reference is to the physical body, the mortal body, viewed as the arena in which sin resides and wages its warfare. He longs to be liberated from a body in which he experiences the effects of sin, and which is destined to die.[27]

It is important to understand what Paul means by the phrase 'the body of death'. Three very different views have been offered.

The first view understands Paul to refer to man's body as the vehicle through which he expresses his sinfulness and rebellion against God; the cry for deliverance then becomes the cry of an unconverted man for redemption. It relates to justification rather than sanctification or glorification. According to this view, Paul has in mind the physical body, considered as the principal instrument by which sin subjugates the soul and plunges it into a state of spiritual death, alienation from God and the life of sin.

Ridderbos thus argues that what is involved 'is not the body as material organism, as though the new life could only reveal itself in man when he had laid aside, indeed had independently "put to death" his present corporeality'. According to Ridderbos, what is intended is 'the sinful mode of existence of man'. This is in harmony with his view that the discord pictured in Romans 7 consists in 'the absolute impotence of the I to break through the barrier of sin and the flesh in any degree at all'.[28]

Käsemann argues for a similar view since, according to him, Paul throughout the passage has been speaking not of ethical conflict, but of 'possession and destiny', of mankind sold under sin, of 'lost mankind'. Paul is understood to be dealing with the salvation of the sinner rather than the sanctification of the saint throughout this passage. Accordingly, when dealing with verse 24 Käsemann writes, 'What remains is only the lament and the cry for redemption. Thereupon our creatureliness is, so to speak, shrivelled up. What is brought to light is the depth of our fall, not our relatedness to God.'

According to this view the lament and cry for deliverance in verse 24 are held to confirm the 'sold under sin' of verse 14. 'The Christian understands it as an expression of the sighing of every creature, as the truth of real human being to which the true God responds by accomplishing the freedom of the bound, deliverance from the compulsion by cosmic forces, and the justification of the godless. Only the Christian can see it thus, since he is rescued from the power of the illusion which rules the world under Adam.'[29]

Despite the attractiveness of the energetic presentation of the Reformed doctrine of justification which undergirds this understanding of verse 24, I believe it is quite simply not what Paul has in mind as he pens this verse. We have seen that throughout this passage he is speaking not about justification, but of the life of the Christian. The above interpretation fits badly into its context, both in this chapter and the wider context of the developing theme of the epistle.

According to a second interpretation, 'the body of death' is viewed to mean the whole mass or burden of sin which weighs so heavily on the believer's heart. Calvin writes, 'He [Paul] calls the body of death the mass of sin, the lump from which the whole man is formed, except that in him those remains only continued by the bonds of which he was kept a captive.'[30]

Such a view is entirely consistent with an overall understanding of the passage as applying to believers. In addition unquestionably the apostle longed to be rid of sin in all its forms and consequences. Thus far such commentators are absolutely right. Such a longing is implied in the cry for deliverance. We may not, however, divest the phrase of its physical connotation. Here, as in chapter 6:6, Paul is referring to his physical body as the arena in which sin manifests itself, a literal body composed of various members (7:23), a 'mortal body' (6:12), 'the body of sin', characterized by sin (6:6).

According to a third view, the 'body' is viewed, as in the first interpretation, as the vehicle through which man expresses his sinfulness. But now Paul is held to be saying that the connection between sin and the body is so close, even in the experience of the Christian (which is the subject of the passage), that the only possible way to be rid of the effects of remaining sin is to be rid of the body. So Cranfield writes, 'That from which the speaker longs to be delivered is the condition of life in the body as we know it under the occupation of sin which has just been described, a life which, because of sin, must succumb to death.'[31]

We may go even further and agree with those who, following the interpretation of Chrysostom, take the word 'body' in its fullest physical sense. Chrysostom saw in Paul's cry a longing for physical death. 'For how long am I obliged to live in this miserable body?' This is an interpretation which makes good sense, and fits the grammar and syntax perfectly.

The deliverance bestowed by Christ, for which the wretched man longs, is more than deliverance from sin's power. What he desires is deliverance 'out of *[ek]* the body of this death', that is, this mortal body which at present is the place where sin resides (7:23). Packer writes convincingly when he says, 'But that deliverance will not come until "this mortal shall have put on immortality" (1 Cor. 15:54): a consummation for which, according to Romans 8:23, those who have the Spirit wait, groaning. And it is surely this groaning, in exact terms, which Romans 7:24 voices. What the "wretched man" is longing for is what 8:23 calls "the redemption of our body". But, if this is so, then what he gives thanks for in v. 25a must be the promise that through Christ this blessing will ultimately be his.'[32]

When the longings of the wretched man in verse 24 are viewed in this way, as merely the articulation of the believer's longing after perfect holiness, which parallel both the groaning of the whole of creation, and the believer's inward groaning after the redemption of the body, then the passage becomes entirely comprehensible. There is no need to view it as a literary device, nor must a construction be forced upon it which ill befits the context. Perfect holiness will be experienced only when the believer exchanges his present mortal body for the heavenly body with which he will be clad one day. Paul expresses this longing to be clad with a heavenly dwelling very beautifully in 2 Corinthians 5:1-5: 'Now we know that if the earthly tent we live in is destroyed, we have a building from God, an eternal house in heaven, not built by human hands. Meanwhile we groan, longing to be clothed with our heavenly dwelling, because when we are clothed, we will not be found naked. For while we are in this tent, we groan and are burdened, because we do not wish to be unclothed but to be clothed with our heavenly dwelling, so that what is mortal may be swallowed up by life. Now it is God who has made us for this very purpose and has given us the Spirit as a deposit, guaranteeing what is to come.'

The very conflict and longing, as expressed in Romans 7, are provoked by the Holy Spirit, as he causes us to aspire after our new clothing, the glorified bodies prepared for us by Christ.

The saint's aspiration after glory is well portrayed in Horatius Bonar's beautiful hymn. It is to our shame that we long so little for Christ's return in power.

> My God, it is not fretfulness
> That makes me say 'How long?'
> It is not heaviness of heart
> That hinders me in song;
> 'Tis not despair of truth and right,
> Nor coward dreams of wrong.
>
> But how can I, with such a hope
> Of glory and of home;
> With such a joy before my eyes,
> Not wish the time were come—
> Of years the jubilee, of days
> The Sabbath and the sum?
>
> These years, what ages they have been!
> This life, how long it seems!
> And how can I, in evil days,
> 'Mid unknown hills and streams,
> But sigh for those of home and heart,
> And visit them in dreams?
>
> Yet peace, my heart; and hush, my tongue;
> Be calm, my troubled breast;
> Each restless hour is hastening on
> The everlasting rest:
> Thou knowest that the time thy God
> Appoints for thee, is best.

Let faith, not fear nor fretfulness,
Awake the cry, 'How long?'
Let not faint-heartedness of soul
Damp thy aspiring song:
Right comes, truth dawns, the night departs
Of error and of wrong.

'Thanks be to God — through Jesus Christ our Lord!' (7:25)

This is Paul's response to the heart-rending cry of verse 24. It expresses triumphantly his assurance of ultimate deliverance from this body of death, and from the captivity to the law of sin which had occasioned his anguished complaint. The answer follows immediately upon the formulation of the question, thereby showing that Paul did not phrase the question in forlorn hope and from the depths of despair.

Throughout this chapter, Paul has indicated the inability of the law to deliver him. As we saw earlier, that was precisely the theme of the chapter. The law can neither justify a sinner, nor sanctify a saint, He has expressed poignantly the depth of his need, as he grappled with the fact and ghastliness of the relics of sin in his believing heart, and depicted the intensity of the spiritual warfare provoked by the Holy Spirit's abiding presence within him. But at no time has he intimated despair of deliverance. He was already aware of who had delivered him from the condemnation of sin, despite the inability of the law; and he also knew who would pursue and perfect that good work, and deliver from the body of this death. He therefore hastens exultingly to proclaim deliverance 'through Jesus Christ our Lord'.

In this triumphant expression Paul thanks God for the assurance of full and final victory through Christ over the consequences of sin. He uses the full title of the Mediator through whom victory is assured, describing his person, 'Jesus', his office, 'Christ' (the Anointed One) and his relation to us, 'Lord'. When and how this triumph will take place is not here disclosed. That is reserved for the next chapter (8:11,17,21,23), but already the certainty of victory is a cause for gratitude and rejoicing.

The passage finds clear parallels elsewhere in Paul. In 1 Corinthians 15:57 the apostle again expresses his thankfulness for assured victory. 'Thanks be to God! He gives us the victory through our Lord Jesus Christ.' It is beyond question that the hope referred to in this passage is that of physical resurrection. Similarly in Philippians 3:21 Paul writes, 'We eagerly await a Saviour from [heaven], the Lord Jesus Christ, who, by the power that enables him to bring everything under his control, will transform our lowly bodies so that they will be like his glorious body.' It is not unreasonable to suppose that in Romans 7 Paul is referring to the same glorious hope, particularly since in the following chapter he proceeds to speak of inward groanings 'as we wait eagerly for our adoption as sons, the redemption of our bodies' (8:23).

It is unwarranted to assume that the cry of triumph of verse 25 expresses gratitude for victory already experienced, and to conclude on this assumption that the writer must have justification in mind. This assumption has been responsible for a great deal of confusion in the exegesis of the passage. It is inconsistent with what Paul proceeds to say in 8:10: 'But if Christ is in you, your body is dead because of sin, yet your spirit is alive because of righteousness. And if the Spirit of him who raised Jesus from the dead is living in you, he who raised Christ from the dead will also give life to your mortal bodies through his Spirit, who lives in you.' The apostle's thought has moved on from justification to glorification, the latter being only the completion of sanctification.

Cranfield is surely right when he states, 'The implication of 25a then is not that the speaker has been delivered "out of the body of this death", but that he knows that God will surely deliver him from it in the future. Deliverance in the limited sense of separation from the body could come with death, deliverance in all its positive fulness would come with the eschatological redemption of the body of death, "the redemption of our bodies" (8:23).'[33]

'So then, I myself in my mind am a slave to God's law, but in the sinful nature a slave to the law of sin' (7:25).

Those who understand the first part of verse 25 to be the cry of an unregenerate man for justification, or of an 'unspiritual Christian' for sanctification, have great difficulty in fitting this second part of the verse into their exegesis. After the climactic affirmation of victory and deliverance in the first part of the verse comes a confession of continuing slavery. Having led the reader to the pinnacle of triumph, instead of immediately striding victoriously into the great affirmations of chapter 8, as would have been the logical step, Paul returns to the description of struggle of the previous verses. And the condition of the speaker after his deliverance is exactly the same as it was before.

One attempt to solve the problem is to suggest a rearrangement of the text in order to make Paul's statement fit a theory. The order of the verses would be rearranged to read 23, 25b, 24, 25a. This is the suggestion of commentators like Moffatt, Dodd, Müller and Michael, but it is surely 'a ploy of last resort'.

Another suggested explanation is that the second part of verse 25 was not part of the original text, but was added as a gloss, summarizing verses 15-23, and should therefore be omitted from the text. This, however, is a purely arbitrary suggestion, for there is not a scrap of textual evidence to support the idea that it is a gloss. All the evidence shows it to be an integral part of the original text.

A further attempt to solve the problem is to understand the phrase 'I myself' as meaning something other than its normal usage. In passages such as Luke 24:39; Romans 9:3; 2 Corinthians 10:1; Romans 15:14 and 2 Corinthians 12:13, the speaker or writer wishes simply to draw attention to himself. Sanday, Headlam and Denney construct the phrase to mean, 'I myself apart from Jesus Christ,' or 'I when left to my own resources', or 'I left to myself', or again, 'I apart from grace'. Such a view understands Paul to mean that he, Paul, left to himself, would still be in the position already described. According to this view the latter part of verse 25 does not describe the actual condition of the man who has been delivered (for he has not been left to himself), but what his condition would still be, had it not been for God's intervention.

A variation of this exegesis is the view of Mitton, who builds his whole exegesis on these two words. He applies the phrase not just to the unregenerate person requiring justification, but also to the regenerate person who backslides. For him the chapter describes both the miserable past from which the Christian has been delivered, and 'the miserable present' into which he may fall again if he tries to stand in his own strength.

The great difficulty with this explanation in both its forms is that it reads into 'I myself' something that is not there.

'The natural rendering of these words is "I, even I", "I myself".

This is very different from "I thrown on my own resources", or, "I, left to myself", "I alone without Christ". We must not import into the phrase something which it does not contain. Elsewhere in Scriptures the phrase carries its natural translation.'[34]

The extent to which commentators who propose the above views are aware of the awkwardness of the sentence in the second part of verse 25 is typified by Käsemann's remarkably honest, yet extraordinary conclusion. Arguing for the view that the sentence should be viewed as a gloss, he writes, 'How precarious it is to assert there is a gloss here against the whole textual tradition merely on material grounds cannot be minimized in the slightest. There is no historical evidence for this. On the other hand, the price which has to be paid for assuming authenticity should not be underestimated. For in this case it is not just our interpretation of the context which falls. All that Paul says about baptism, law and the justification of the ungodly, namely, all that he says about the break between the aeons, will have to be interpreted differently... The material problem is not solved by putting the sentence after verse 23. Here if anywhere we have a gloss of a later reader which presents the first Christian interpretation of verses 17-24.'[35]

The alternative to such an unwarranted and artificial solution is to adopt the Christian interpretation as outlined in our exposition above. If we do so the sentence in question is not at all awkward, but fits perfectly into the whole paragraph. Once it is recognized that the person who speaks is a Christian (and a mature Christian — not merely one who is still on a specially low level of Christian experience), and also that the first part of the verse expresses, not consciousness of having already been delivered 'out of the body of this death', but certainty that God will in the future deliver him from it, a straightforward and satisfactory interpretation of the latter part of the verse becomes possible. Far from being an anticlimax or an incongruous intrusion at this point, it is an altogether appropriate conclusion to the preceding verses (including verses 24 and 25a). With great intensity Paul longs for final deliverance, which in due time God will grant him. But with great honesty he depicts the real anguish in his heart as he awaits the day. There is no complacent acceptance of the imperfections of his present life, caused by remaining sin within him. Rather there is eager longing for the redemption of the body. With the phrase 'I myself' Paul does not mean to draw attention to the fact that he is speaking about himself.

Rather he shows how the believer is engaged in the very depths of his being in the service of the law of God, as one who is being renewed by the Holy Spirit. But this does not cloak the painful fact of the Christian's continuing sinfulness. For this reason Paul goes on frankly to acknowledge that the believer, so long as he remains in this present life, remains in a real (though limited) sense a slave of sin, since he still lives in the flesh.

The man in Christ serves the law of God with his mind, in the sense that in his new spiritual nature he desires to keep it perfectly; but with the flesh he serves the law of sin, as appears from the fact that he is never able to keep the law as consistently and perfectly as he wishes to do. As long as this life lasts, there continues the tension between the old and the new, between the heart and the members in the life of the Christian. This is the explanation of Paul's cry. As long as he lives 'in the flesh', and is thus a member in the body of death, which mankind is under Adam its head, there remains the tension between being 'in Christ' and being 'in the flesh'. The emphatic 'I myself', or 'I, even I', expresses Paul's sense of how painfully paradoxical it is that a Christian man like himself, who desires so heartily to keep God's law and do only good, should find himself under the constant necessity of breaking the law and doing what in effect is sin. But such is the state of the Christian until his body is redeemed. Hence the longing for the eschatological deliverance through which the tension between his longing and his achievement will be abolished.

Conclusion

The exegesis offered above is, I believe, entirely compatible with the immediate context. In these verses, 7:14-25, there is nothing said which is inconsistent with a regenerate man's experience, while several expressions are inconsistent with the unregenerate state. The view taken also fits perfectly into the wider context, where Paul has been showing that, just as observance of the law is inadequate to produce justification, so observance of the law is incapable of sanctifying the Christian. But both are obtainable by the believer, indeed are assured to the believer, 'through Jesus Christ our Lord'.

César Malan (1787-1864) beautifully portrays the triumph

associated with being delivered out the body of this death when he writes the following lines:

> It is not death to die,
> To leave this weary road,
> And, midst the brotherhood on high,
> To be at home with God.
>
> It is not death to close,
> The eye long dimmed by tears,
> And wake in glorious repose,
> To spend eternal years.
>
> It is not death to bear
> The wrench that sets us free
> From dungeon chain, to breathe the air
> Of boundless liberty.
>
> It is not death to fling
> Aside this sinful dust,
> And rise on strong exulting wing
> To live among the just.
>
> Jesus, thou Prince of Life!
> Thy chosen cannot die;
> Like thee, they conquer in the strife,
> To reign with thee on high.

The same sentiment is expressed from a slightly different angle by Henry Alford (1810-71):

> Ten thousand times ten thousand,
> In sparkling raiment bright,
> The armies of the ransomed saints
> Throng up the steeps of light;
> 'Tis finished, all is finished,
> Their fight with death and sin;
> Fling open wide the golden gates,
> And let the victors in.

What rush of hallelujahs
Fills all the earth and sky!
What ringing of a thousand harps
Bespeaks the triumph nigh!
O day for which creation
and all its tribes were made!
O joy, for all its former woes
A thousandfold repaid!

Bring near thy great salvation,
Thou Lamb for sinners slain;
Fill up the roll of thine elect,
Then take thy power and reign;
Appear, Desire of nations,
Thine exiles long for home;
Show in the heavens thy promised sign;
Thou Prince and Saviour, come.

4.
Paraphrase of Romans 7:14-25

What is the explanation of the impotence of the law to produce the good?

v.14. Clearly it is not the fault of the law for, as all believers know, the law is spiritual. It was given by God the Holy Spirit, has therefore divine authority and exercises a spiritual ministry in the human heart. The problem is myself. When I compare myself with the spiritual law of God, and consider the perfect inward as well as outward purity it requires, I am aware of lack of conformity to its holiness, and am convicted of my sinfulness. Even though regenerate, I am far from the holiness of heart this spiritual law requires. I am carnal. By this I mean, not that I am entirely or exclusively under the control of the flesh, nor an immature believer, but as someone still living in the body of sinful flesh, I am well aware of the relics of sin which still remain in my life. The flesh, that corrupt source and principle of evil, though deprived of its dominion, still remains in me, with much force and activity. Though by God's grace I am not like Ahab, who with full determination of his heart abandoned himself fully to work evil, yet the flesh, with its violent corrupt affections and unholy passions, often carries me away as a captive and slave, contrary to the habitual and prevailing inclination of my heart and will.

v.15. I do not condone this inconsistent behaviour. Unfortunately what my will inclines me to do, by its habitual determination, I do not always succeed in doing. This is because I am obstructed by the flesh and the weakness which remaining corruption brings upon me. I truly and sincerely hate sin, but sadly that is what I too often do.

v.16. This habitual inclination of my will (despite my aberrations, for which I hold myself entirely responsible) shows that I heartily consent to the goodness of the law, that it is good in itself, and prescribes what is good for me, which is conducive to my duty and happiness.

v.17. Though, strictly speaking, it is I who do all that is done by the activity of sin in my heart, and though I cannot justify myself before this holy and spiritual law, nor claim that I am not responsible for it (the whole problem is my double situation, being in Christ, but still in the flesh), yet grace allows me to take some comfort by saying that it is not I myself who do the evil, which I sincerely hate, and is so contrary to the habitual inclination of my will, but my most hateful enemy sin, which continues its habitation, though not its dominion, in me.

v.18. It is grace that enables me to make this distinction. I am fully aware that apart from what the grace of God has accomplished in me, nothing good is found in me. By this I mean that in my flesh (that is in myself apart from grace, as I am by nature, and to the extent that my sinful nature has not yet been perfectly renewed), I know nothing good is to be found.

v.19. For what I do is not the whole good that my will is fully bent on and inclined to: no, the evil I do not want to do, which is contrary to the fixed determination of my will, keeps springing up within me, through remaining corruption, and this is what I keep on doing.

v.20. Now as a man's moral character is to be taken from the sincere habitual inclination of his heart and will, and if it is under the influence of the flesh that I do what is contrary to the spiritual and holy law, and what my will is averse to, then, it is not I (let me again encourage myself with the thought), it is not my very self who does it, but sin living in me.

v.21. Let me recapitulate what I have been saying. I find a strong effective principle of action working within me: that when I want to do the right, wrong suggestions crowd in and prevent me from doing good.

v.22. If you ask how it is possible that when the will is determined to do good, evil can still be present, the answer is that there are two antithetical laws that affect me. On the one hand, there is the law of God, in which in my inmost being I take great delight.

v.23. But while with my whole heart I delight in the holiness of this spiritual law of God, I see another, very different law present in my corrupt nature and manifesting itself through my physical members. This law, or principle, within me wages war against the law of God which I love in my inmost self, and which regulates my mind, and my mind serves. This second principle which is present in my corrupt nature not only battles against the law of God, which is written indelibly in my heart by the Spirit of God; it works hard, and, alas! with far too much success in some particular instances, to captivate me to the law of sin which manifests itself through my physical members.

v.24. What a miserable distressing condition in which to find myself! It really distresses me to think of such inconsistencies in the life of a believer, especially when the whole longing of my heart is for inner holiness, as described in God's holy and spiritual law. Who will liberate me from this bondage? When will I ever be free from this physical body though which sin manifests itself, this condition of life in the body I have just described, a life which, because of the remnants of sin in this present earthly existence and evil age, must succumb to death? What I am longing for is not forgiveness or justification. I want to be delivered out of this mortal body, which is at present sin's place of residence. But who will deliver me? The law is certainly impotent to do so. Is there no liberator?

v.25. Thank God, there is ! Through the Lord Jesus Christ I have complete assurance of full and final victory over all the consequences of sin. One day Christ, who triumphed over sin, and rose physically, will redeem my body too. This mortal body will put on immortality. Through the Lord Jesus Christ I will be fully and finally freed from sin in every form.

Meanwhile, however, there continues the struggle I have described above. So long as this life lasts, there continues the tension between the old age and the new, between my renewed self and the relics of sin within my members. With my mind, through that good and prevailing law which divine grace has put in my mind and heart, I myself wholeheartedly, truly and sincerely (though still imperfectly) serve the law of God, though, alas! with my sinful nature, the cause of my greatest sorrow, I serve the law of sin.

5.
Important principles of sanctification

Having attempted to understand Romans 7 in its general context in the epistle, and having examined the text itself in some detail, we are now in a position to make some observations regarding the practical implications of the passage for the doctrine of sanctification. It is beyond the scope of this study to present any detailed exposition of the doctrine of sanctification, but I consider the following principles to be of capital importance.

Regeneration leads to holiness

Firstly, it is unwise to make too strong a distinction between justification and regeneration on the one hand, and sanctification on the other, as if they are totally isolated and unconnected experiences. While they are clearly distinguishable aspects of the Christian life, they are always found together, the one being the concomitant of the other. Thus in this epistle we have seen how Paul's thought flows from justification to its inevitable implications for personal holiness. Regeneration and sanctification are not separate experiences, but are related as seed is to fruit. If the tree is good the fruit will be good. In other words, regeneration produces holiness, and holiness presupposes regeneration. There is no instant leap from immaturity to maturity in the Christian life, but rather spiritual growth and development, as elsewhere in organic life.

The great weakness in 'higher-life' theories of sanctification is that they underestimate the significance of regeneration. They imply that there is a lower level of Christian life and experience where believers know only defeat and frustration, and from which they can be delivered only through a second definitive experience of divine grace, the gift of sanctification. Many Christians have been haunted by this concept of a two-stage, or two-tier Christian life so prevalent today, and have inevitably been led into confusion and frustration as they sought for an experience of spiritual crisis which would instantly and irrevocably lead them to life on a higher plane. Sensitive and sincere souls who long and pray to be the best that they can possibly be for God, and to know all the fulness of spiritual blessing that it is possible for a child of God to know on this earth, are often attracted by a teaching that offers more than the minimal Christianity which predominates today. And often in so far as they seek for God, he is pleased to bless them. That, however, does not make their formulation of the doctrine true, and they soon discover that the blessing they have experienced has not raised them beyond the reach of temptation and sin. This in turn can lead to great disillusionment and despondency. One suspects that on other occasions many who spuriously professed faith in Christ under the great emotional pressure of superficial evangelism, but who subsequently were brought by God to true repentance and faith, have been led falsely to define their second experience in terms of 'higher-life sanctification', when in fact it was only the initial glorious, life-transforming spiritual work of regeneration and conversion.

We must not underestimate the vital importance of regeneration. By the effectual call of the Spirit of God, so mysterious and ineffable in his operation, a great comprehensive supernatural work of God is performed in the life of a poor sinner. He is enabled not only to embrace Christ freely as he is offered to him in the gospel, but also to partake of all the benefits of the children of God: justification, adoption and all the blessings which flow from them. In 1 Corinthians 1:30 Paul states that Jesus Christ is made unto us wisdom, righteousness, sanctification and redemption (or final glorification). All of these blessings together comprise salvation, not just one or two. So in Romans 8:30 the golden chain of salvation is seen to be composed of several links. 'Those he predestined, he also called; those he called, he also justified; those he justified, he also glorified.' There is no possibility of a break in the chain from one link to the next. When God calls sinners effectually, he calls them from sin and the world to holiness and to glory. Ezekiel speaks of regeneration as the removal from the sinner of his stony heart and the giving of a heart of flesh. In addition God promises, 'I will put my Spirit in you and move you to follow my decrees, and be careful to keep my laws' (36:26,27). In regeneration, then, the heart and the will are both renewed. The sinner, by God's almighty power, is not only effectually drawn to Christ, being made willing by his grace, but also determined by that same power to do that which is good. How profound and diffusive then is God's supernatural work of regeneration! The principle of new life is implanted in man so that thereafter the governing disposition of the soul is made holy. He is born again, and henceforth his new life manifests itself. He bears fruit unto holiness. The tree is made good, and the fruit assured.

We have seen how in Romans 6 Paul answers the taunts of antinomians by indicating this very principle: 'Shall we continue in sin...? Certainly not! You have died, been buried, been raised... Sin therefore shall not have dominion over you.' The notion of a Christian being permanently defeated and overwhelmed by sin is totally preposterous. By definition he has been raised to newness of life. Christ's triumph assures his victory.

Inner conflict is part of the Christian life

Secondly, the Christian who is maturing and being sanctified experiences much inner conflict. He has been definitively sanctified at regeneration (1 Cor. 1:2,30), but thereafter he is engaged in a process of maturing, which involves much inner struggle. It is wrong to suggest that he experiences no fightings, no struggling against sin, but that rather through one conscious act of 'yielding to God', of 'letting go and letting God', as our Perfectionist Christian friends sometimes put it, we achieve instant permanent victory. The teaching of Romans 7 is quite the reverse: 'Offer yourselves to God,' exhorts Paul in chapter 6:13; this does not mean passively placing ourselves in the hands of another, but actively presenting ourselves and all our faculties for service (Rom. 12:1-2). There is a holy violence, conflict, warfare, struggle and fight in the Christian's life. We are called as soldiers to engage in combat, as athletes to wrestle, struggle and run the race. There is much to attract in the sensationalism of 'instant holiness', with its rousing, exciting Christianity. But crisis sanctification is not biblical sanctification, indeed is not sanctification at all. It supplants the need for self-examination, mortification and constant growth in grace.

Those who reject the application of Romans 7:14-25 to believers on the grounds that such expressions of anguish and turmoil are incompatible with the experience of regeneration are clearly wrong, as passages such as Galatians 5:17 prove: 'For the flesh desires what is contrary to the Spirit, and the Spirit what is contrary to the flesh. They are in conflict with each other, so that you do not do what you want.'

The depth of sin in the heart

Thirdly, we see in Romans 7 how deep are the roots of sin in the human heart and how great are its force and activity in the hearts even of the best of men. It is not just deep-rooted habits that the Christian has to oppose, but a corrupted and depraved nature which, though defeated, still causes the believer indescribable anguish and trouble. The apostle Paul has a strong doctrine of original sin. Its roots are so deep in human nature as never to be wholly eradicated in this life. Though the apostle might be preserved from remarkable lapses in outward practice, the principle of sin, while defeated, remains active and finds occasion to manifest itself through his members. So long as the believer lives on earth, with all the limitations of this present evil age which that implies, so long will he be caused to grieve over the presence of remaining sin in his life, despite his being raised with Christ, and his belonging already in some measure to the age to come.

The deliverance from the power of sin secured by union with Christ, and from the defilement of sin secured by regeneration, does not eliminate all sin from the heart and life of the believer. There is still indwelling sin. This being so, there must be the conflict which Paul describes in Romans 7.

The work of the Spirit

Fourthly, the passage clearly teaches that sanctification is produced not through works of the law, but by the Holy Spirit, through the risen and glorified Christ. At times Reformed theology is guilty of stressing the means of grace rather than the Spirit as the author of holiness. We must be careful to maintain the biblical balance.

The Scriptures teach that believers are so united to Christ that they are partakers not only of his death, but also of his Holy Spirit, who dwells in them as a principle of life. He brings them more and more into conformity with the image of God and works in them both to will and to do according to his own good pleasure. The Bible teaches that, so long as men are under the law — that is, trying to gain acceptance with God by satisfying the demands of the law — their attempts are doomed to frustration and failure. A legal spirit expresses a sense of duty and fear of punishment, but this is the experience of slaves, not sons. Legalism does not produce right feelings towards God, any more that it produces the fruits of holiness. When, however, by the death of Christ, sinners are freed from the law as a means of righteousness, their whole relation to God is changed. They are no longer slaves, but sons. Being united to Christ in his death, they are partakers of his life, and in virtue of this union they bring forth fruit unto God. They are henceforth led by the Spirit who dwells in them (Rom. 7:4-6).

The doctrine of sanctification, therefore, as taught in the Bible, is that we are made holy, not by force of conscience or moral motives, nor by acts of discipline, but by being united to Christ. That is the great distinctive Christian teaching of holiness, so different from the morality of other religions. By being united to Christ we are reconciled to God, and made partakers of the Holy Spirit who sanctifies us. This is the explanation of Paul's assured reply to his own question in Romans 7:24: 'Who will rescue me from this body of death? Thanks be to God through Jesus Christ our Lord!' Christ is made unto us sanctification as well as justification (1 Cor. 1:30). He not only frees from the penalty of the law, but makes us holy. There is therefore, according to the gospel, no such thing as sanctification without, or before, or separate from justification. Those who are outside of Christ are under the power, as well as under the condemnation of sin; and those who are in Christ are not only free from condemnation, but also delivered from the dominion of sin. This is the truth which is highlighted in Romans chapters 7 and 8. 'Through Jesus Christ the law of the Spirit of life set me free from the law of sin and death' (8:2). While the Holy Spirit is not specifically mentioned in chapter 7:14-25, his activity is implied throughout as the one who provokes the conflict, and will answer our longings. The matter is made explicit in the following chapter when Paul declares, 'We, ourselves, who have the first-fruits of the Spirit, groan inwardly as we wait eagerly for our adoption as sons, the redemption of our bodies' (8:23).

It is necessary to be reminded that we do not sanctify ourselves. It is God who sanctifies (1 Thess. 5:23). This he does through the agency of the Holy Spirit. It is imperative that we realize our dependence upon the Holy Spirit. We must not forget, of course, that our activity is enlisted to the fullest extent in the process of sanctification. But we must not rely upon our own strength of resolution and purpose. It is when we are weak that we are strong. It is by grace that we are being saved, as surely as it is by grace that we have been saved. If we are not keenly sensitive to our own helplessness, then we can make the use of the means of sanctification the minister of self-righteousness and pride, and thus defeat the end of sanctification. We must not rely upon the means of sanctification, but upon God himself, the God of all grace. Self-confident moralism promotes pride, while sanctification promotes humility and contrition. The complaint of Romans 7:24 is of the essence of holiness.

Sanctification is not the product of human effort, but the purchase of Jesus Christ for his people. Christ is made unto us sanctification (1 Cor. 1:30). This is mediated to us through the Holy Spirit. But the Spirit does not act without reference to Christ. As there is unity in the Godhead, so there is unity in the divine activity of sanctification. It is as the Spirit of Christ, and as the Spirit of him who raised Christ from the dead, that the Holy Spirit sanctifies. Murray rightly says, 'We may not think of the Spirit as operative in us apart from the risen and glorified Christ. The sanctifying process is not only dependent upon the death and resurrection of Christ in its initiation; it is dependent upon the death and resurrection of Christ in its continuance. It is by the efficacy and virtue which proceed from the exalted Lord that sanctification is carried on, and such virtue belongs to the exalted Lord by reason of his death and resurrection. It is by the Spirit that this virtue is communicated... The sanctifying work of the Spirit not only consists in progressive conformation to the image of Christ, but is also dependent upon the activity of the exalted Lord (cf. 1 Cor. 15:45). It is the peculiar prerogative of the Holy Spirit to glorify Christ by taking the things of Christ and showing them unto the people of God (cf. John

16:14,16; 2 Cor. 3:17,18). It is as the indwelling Spirit that he does this and as the advocate with believers (John 14:17).[1]

It is at this point that chapters 6, 7 and 8 of Romans coincide. In chapter 6 the work of Christ is shown to result inevitably in the believer's victory over sin. In chapter 7 we see how the Holy Spirit provokes conflict in the believer's heart, as he takes the things of Christ and reveals them to him in a way that causes him to mourn over the sin which remains within him. Then in chapter 8 we find life in the Spirit overcoming all obstacles, even death, and giving the assurance that nothing can ever separate the Christian from Christ's love. Christ at the beginning, Christ in the middle, Christ at the end — and all through the Spirit. It is thus that God initiates, pursues and consummates his glorious work in the lives of his people.

Sanctification is the work of God. It is not a programme of human self-improvement or an automatic process. God must do it. God alone can do it. And God will do it! We are totally dependent upon the energizing activity of the Spirit, as he takes of the things of Christ and reveals them to us.

The responsibility of the individual

Fifthly, sanctification is an experience for which every Christian is responsible. While we are constantly and wholly dependent upon the supernatural agency of the Holy Spirit, we must remind ourselves that sanctification is not something that takes place outside of our consciousness, or beyond our conscious activity. In all his dealings with us God treats us as persons, not inanimate objects. He is not a great Procrustean deity who rains blessings down upon an unwilling people. We are not pawns but living, active persons. In blessing us God draws out and enlists to the full our active participation in a life of holiness. We are not passive in this great process of sanctification.

This principle of Christian response and activity is clearly implied in Romans 7. Paul longs to do good, is totally committed to obey the law of God, to such an extent indeed that he speaks of himself as a slave in service to God's law (7:25). There is no quietism here, but an active engagement in the service of God. There is no defeatist attitude with regard to sin. This positive element is further developed in chapter 8, where it is stated that the practical effects of God's sending the law were 'in order that the righteous requirements of the law might be fully met in us, who do not live according to the sinful nature but according to the Spirit' (8.4). Calvin is right when he insists that sanctification is not just a theme for discussion but a reality which can be observed: 'The goal of our regeneration is that there might be seen in our life a harmony and accord between the justice of God and our obedience... The gospel is not a doctrine of speech, but of life.'[2]

It is for this reason that Paul exhorts the Philippian church to work out their salvation with fear and trembling as God works within them to will and to do according to God's good pleasure (Phil. 2:12-13). God works, and as a result we work. The activity of the one, rather than suspending the activity of the other, in fact promotes it. John Murray, commenting on this passage, remarks, 'The more persistently active we are in working, the more persuaded we may be that all the energizing grace and power is of God.'[3]

In the case of sanctification, as in that of regeneration, respect must be paid to human responsibility as well as divine sovereignty. Salvation is by grace, which is sovereign and received through faith that, though a gift, is exercised personally by the sinner. It is similar with regard to sanctification. God determines the end — holiness, or conformity to the image of Christ. He also determines the means to that end — the work of the Spirit in drawing out our hearts after Christ and enlisting our response in prayer, obedience, mortification of sin, engagement in spiritual warfare and the use of all the means of grace.

Godliness involves the engagement of heart, mind and will, and the use of all the means of grace established by the Lord. Holiness is always associated with prayerfulness, delight in God's Word, diligent use of the means of grace, joyful obedience, spiritual warfare and a ravished delight in the Lord as we frequent the throne of grace. Yet we must recognize that the means of grace are effectual only in so far as they are truly spiritual activities which lead to Christ. Without the energizing power of the Holy Spirit they degenerate into formalism, mysticism, pietism, sacramentalism, or barren intellectualism.

Samuel Longfellow (1819-92) well expresses this balance between divine and human activity in sanctification in his lovely hymn:

Holy Spirit, truth divine,
Dawn upon this soul of mine;
Word of God, and inward light,
Wake my spirit, clear my sight.

Holy Spirit, love divine,
Glow within this heart of mine;
Kindle every high desire.
Perish self in thy pure fire.

Holy Spirit, power divine,
Fill and nerve this will of mine;
By thee may I strongly live,
Bravely bear, and nobly strive.

So, too, does Joseph Hart (1712-68):

Cheer our desponding hearts
Thou heavenly Paraclete;
Give us to lie with humble hope
At our Redeemer's feet.

'Tis thine to cleanse the heart,
To sanctify the soul,
To pour fresh life in every part,
And new create the whole.

No 'perfectionism'

Sixthly, it is unwise when speaking of sanctification to use the vague language of 'perfectionism'. It is true that believers are exhorted to '[perfect] holiness in the fear of God' (2 Cor. 7:1, NKJV), to 'go on unto perfection' (Heb. 6:1, NKJV), or maturity (NIV), to 'aim for perfection', or 'become complete' (2 Cor. 13:11). But Scripture nowhere teaches that a literal perfection, freedom from sin, in thought, word and deed, is attained by any child of Adam in this life. Indeed the greatest saints throughout all ages have had the greatest sense of their own unworthiness; we need only think of David, John, Rutherford, M'Cheyne and Baxter. John reminds us that 'If we claim to be without sin, we deceive ourselves, and the truth is not in us' (1 John 1:8).

The corporate aspect

We must also bear in mind that sanctification has a corporate aspect. God's great purpose of grace involves not just the sanctification of individuals, but the sanctification and glorification of the entire body of believers, the church of the Lord Jesus Christ. This corporate dimension has important practical implications.

It is true that we come to Christ one by one, and that as individuals we are incorporated into Christ. Yet there is great danger of thinking atomistically and of forgetting that God's great design encompasses his whole church. Christ is building the church which is his body. This corporate aspect affects our salvation at every stage of Christian experience — our regeneration, sanctification and final glorification.

When sinners are brought to repentance and faith in Christ, they are spoken of in Scripture as being added to the church. This is a living organism, described under various metaphors. It is the body of which Christ is the Head, the temple of God composed of living stones, a vine of which Christ is the main plant and believers the individual branches, the bride of Christ, the heavenly Bridegroom. Through regeneration and conversion a believer is incorporated into Christ and added to his body. The idea of a Christian remaining outside, unconnected, dislocated from the body, is contrary to Christ's revealed will. Regeneration implies incorporation.

In the same way, sanctification has a corporate aspect. The biblical picture is of the whole church growing, developing and being sanctified together. As the Holy Spirit incorporates believers into Christ, and into his body, they are nourished and edified in such a way that they in turn minister to the whole body so that there is corporate sanctification and effective service.

A primary reason lying behind Paul's writing this letter to the Romans was his concern that, in the racially mixed church in Rome, believers might accept one another so as to be able to build one another up in the faith. He carried a great burden on his heart, both for his own people, the Jews (chs 9-11), and for the Gentiles to whom God had sent him (ch.15). So the apostle calls upon them to consider each other to be members of Christ's body, with the calling to build one another up (14:13; 6:14,19).

God's intention is not that his children should grow in faith and holiness in isolation, but together, as members of a family. Together they form the body of which Christ is the Head. They have been joined together for the well-being of the whole (1 Cor. 12-14). God's purpose is that 'The body of Christ may be built up until we all reach unity in the faith and in the knowledge of the Son of God ... and become mature, attaining to the whole measure of the fulness of Christ... From him the whole body, joined and held together by every supporting ligament, grows and builds itself up in love, as each part does its work' (Eph. 4:12-13,16).

Within the church we receive ministry, discipline and counsel from under-shepherds whom the Lord himself has appointed for our blessing (Eph. 4:9-16). Together with our brothers and sisters, we pray, serve and minister to one another in love. The Lord himself in a special way presences himself among us, sups with us and builds us up, as in his name we minister the one to the other. There 'The whole body, supported and held together by its ligaments and sinews, grows as God causes it to grow' (Col. 2:19). As coals when placed together glow with great heat and produce abundant light, so Christ places us together, with the fire of his Spirit glowing in our hearts. Let us pray that as families of God's people we might know in a very real way the Spirit of Christ among us, and together grow up in him!

Of course, this shared experience of growing up in Christ is not an end in itself; it is in anticipation of our final glorification. Like regeneration and sanctification, our final glorification will also have a corporate aspect. It will not be as isolated individual saints that we shall be glorified. Christ will present the church to himself on that day, not as a motley gathering of isolated individuals, but as the bride, the perfect bride, presented to the heavenly Bridegroom (Eph. 5:25-27). Corporate sanctification will be gloriously consummated in corporate glorification.

The redemption of the body

Finally, we remind ourselves of the glorious truth alluded to in Romans 7:24-25 and expanded in chapter 8 — the doctrine of entire sanctification which will coincide with the redemption of our bodies. 'Who will rescue me from this body of death?' asks Paul. 'Thanks be to God — though Jesus Christ our Lord!' Christ will one day return in triumph and glory to rid his people of every trace of sin.

Meanwhile we may be condemned through the period of this short earthly pilgrimage to experience conflict, as those living in heavenly places in Christ, and yet at the same time still in imperfect bodies and in a poor fallen world. But while 'we ourselves, who have the first-fruits of the Spirit, groan inwardly as we wait eagerly for our adoption as sons, the redemption of our bodies,' we have the assurance that the day of final redemption will surely come, and we shall be delivered from the last relics and vestiges of sin. We shall be delivered, not only from the condemnation, guilt and power of sin, but from its very presence.

This doctrine of perfection, or entire sanctification, is held before us in 1 Thessalonians 5:23: 'May God himself, the God of peace, sanctify you through and through. May your whole spirit, soul and body be kept blameless at the coming of our Lord Jesus Christ. The one who calls you is faithful and he will do it.'

Here, as B. B. Warfield points out in his famous sermon on this text, the apostle is speaking of entire sanctification — spirit, soul *and* body. He does not speak of this as a mere ideal which is unobtainable, 'the forever beckoning standard hanging hopelessly above us'. The important point for us to notice is when this will be obtained — 'at the coming of our Lord Jesus Christ'. The faithfulness of God is the pledge of the believer's perfection. It does not hang on our weak endeavours, but on God's almighty and unfailing faithfulness.

Warfield writes, 'There is no promise of its completion in this life... There is only strong exhortation to ceaseless effort, and strong encouragement by promise of its completion in the end. Men here are not *"comprehensores"* but *"viatores"*. We are fighting the good fight; we are running the race. The prize is yonder.

'Certainly the gradualness of this process ought not to disturb us. It may be inexplicable to us that the Almighty God acts by way of process. But that is revealed to us as his chosen way of operation in every sphere of his work, and should not surprise us here. He could, no doubt, make the soul perfect in the twinkling of an eye; just as he could give us each a perfect body at the very instant of our believing. He does not. The removal of the stains and effects of sin

— in an evil heart and in a sick and dying body — is accomplished in a slow process. We all grow sick and die — though Jesus has taken on his broad shoulders (among the other penalties of sin) all our sicknesses and death itself. And we still struggle with the remainders of indwelling sin; though Jesus has bought for us the sanctifying operations of the Spirit. To us it is a weary process. But it is God's way. And he does all things well. And the weariness of the struggle is illuminated by hope. "After a while!" we may say; "after a while!" Or as Paul puts it, faithful is he that calls us, who also will do it. He will do it! And so, after a while, our spirit, and soul and body shall be made blamelessly perfect, all to be so presented before our Lord at that Day. Let us praise the Lord for the glorious prospect!'[4]

Appendices:
Assessment of alternative views

Appendix I:
Miserable because unbelieving

The first view that we examine is one which has had widespread support over the centuries. Paul, it is held, is quite simply describing the frustrating experience of an unbeliever. As he is confronted with the perfect and spiritual law of God, he becomes aware of the sinfulness of his own heart and life. He writhes in agony. He longs to perform the requirements of God's law, but in his fallen state is unable to do so. His life is dominated by sin. He is therefore wretched indeed. He longs for deliverance from the burden of his guilt and inability. He cries out for deliverance, 'Who will rescue me from this body of death?' The answer is given in terms of the glorious gospel of the grace of God: 'Thanks be to God — through Jesus Christ our Lord!'

This seems an obvious way to understand the passage, and appears to suit perfectly what we know of the gospel as a message of hope for miserable sinners. Salvation is offered to lost mankind through Jesus Christ our Lord.

Many commentators have adhered to this general position. Apart from Pelagians, semi-Pelagians and Arminians, who have seen Romans 7 as reflecting the fundamental opposition of flesh and spirit or reason (a dualism of which the Bible knows nothing), or have viewed man as having an inherent ability to do good, and a free will untrammelled by sin, and therefore able unaided to choose God (a view which Scripture denies, 1 Cor. 2:14), some of Reformed biblical convictions have also held this view. Observing specifically Christian phraseology and vocabulary in the passage, they conclude that the expression of defeat and frustration is couched in Christian terms because the plight of the unregenerate world is viewed through the eyes of one who has come to faith in Christ (the apostle Paul). The burden of Romans 7 is the powerlessness of the law in the struggle against sin, indeed its total inadequacy to vanquish the power of sin. We have before us a description of the burdensome plight hanging over all mankind, even in its piety. The subject is man's state of lostness, and his need to be redeemed from the state of bondage under which the law of God retains him. Our text speaks, not of the state of salvation but of lost humanity. It is the experience of life requiring to be born again, an authentic transcript of Paul's own experience during the period which culminated in his vision on the road to Damascus.

The theme of these verses, according to this view, is held to be the law — what it does do, what it does not do, what it cannot do. The apostle is writing not primarily about himself or his own experience, but about the law and its ministry. The whole of chapter 7 is viewed as relating to one great theme — the function and the limitations of the law. Paul is defending himself against charges that he was dismissing the law, that the law is sin, that the ministry of the law was a ministry of death. So he depicts in the final verses of the chapter a case in which the Holy Spirit is applying the spirituality of the law to an awakened heart and conscience. Through the law the Holy Spirit is convicting of sin. The confessions and agonies are those of a man experiencing intense conviction of sin, aware of his weakness and complete failure, but ignorant of any solution. He is trying to keep the law in his own strength, but cannot. He feels condemned, is convicted of sin, but does not understand the gospel of salvation through the grace of God in Christ. Hence his misery. In Romans 7 everything is directed towards throwing light on man's situation of death, his having been sold under sin, his having been taken captive by the superior power of sin. It is a death situation, hence the agony.

Arguments in favour of this view

1. One strong argument in support of the view that the second part of Romans 7, like the first, depicts the situation of an unbeliever, is found in the stark contrast between chapters 7 and 8. When we pass from chapter 7 to chapter 8 we seem to move into an entirely

different atmosphere, from one world of experience to another, so that we are led to believe that both chapters cannot be describing the same stage of Christian development. In chapter 7, not until we come to verse 25 is there a single expression which belongs to Christianity. The name of Jesus Christ does not appear once. There is no mention of the Holy Spirit. By contrast chapter 8 mentions Jesus Christ three times in the first three verses, and the Holy Spirit is mentioned a dozen times in the first sixteen verses. We appear to be far removed from the heartbreaking defeat and the ineffectual struggle and stalemate of chapter 7. Now the frequent mention of 'I' in chapter 7 gives way to abundant references to the Holy Spirit. We appear to have passed from the law/death situation of chapter 7 into the grace/life situation of chapter 8.

Verse 2 of chapter 8 seems to epitomize the contrast between the two chapters: 'Through Christ Jesus the law of the Spirit of life set me free from the law of sin and death.' Is not the 'law of sin and death' precisely that record of moral defeat outlined in chapter 7, and the freedom which Christ has bestowed (not 'will bestow') freedom from that habitual failure?

2. Another telling argument which appears to support this conclusion is the emphatic 'now' in 8:1. 'Therefore, there is *now* no condemnation for those who are in Christ Jesus.' It is claimed that this must imply a contrast with a state of affairs which is past and gone, such as that described in chapter 7.

3. This contrast between the two chapters seems to be heightened by certain statements and phrases in chapter 7 which appear difficult to harmonize with what Paul has written elsewhere about 'the new man in Christ'. For instance, in 6:22 we read, 'But now that you have been set free from sin and have become slaves to God, the benefit you reap leads to holiness.' The significance of this verse is seen in the emphatic contrast between the 'now' and the 'then' in the previous verse. What benefits did you reap then? But now what fruit, now that you have been set free from sin? The distinction between the two experiences is very clear. But this clear affirmation of the Christian's freedom, it is claimed, is at variance with 7:14 and 7:24, where Paul speaks of himself as 'sold under sin' or 'as a slave to sin', and as a 'wretched man', still apparently needing deliverance from the power of sin. In 7:23 he sees in his members

'another law... making me a prisoner of the law of sin at work in my members'. Now to be brought into captivity to sin and to be sold under sin signify much the same thing, the latter expression seems to suggest becoming a slave of sin in the way that prisoners of war become slaves of victors, while the former expression describes the resultant state of incarceration and bondage. Such language seems far removed from Paul's earlier statements regarding freedom from sin and fruit leading to sanctification. Are such phrases not more easily seen as belonging to the 'then' of 6:21, rather than the 'now' of 6:22?

Further, it is argued that the statement, 'I am carnal,' is the confession of an unregenerate person, under law, and is equivalent to being 'in the flesh', a phrase used in 8:9 to denote a person unquestionably unregenerate and bereft of the Spirit. And is not the outright confession of possessing a will to do good that has no effect in practice totally inconsistent with a state of grace? 'For what I want to do I do not do, but what I hate I do... I have the desire to do what is good, but I cannot carry it out... For what I do is not the good I want to do; no, the evil I do not want to do — this I keep on doing' (7:15,18,19). What sort of Christian experience is this, which is totally ineffectual? Must not the person in question be a stranger to the regenerating work of the Holy Spirit? For in the experience of the truly regenerate heart God works both the willing and the doing (Phil. 2:13). Could a person who had experienced the liberating power of the Spirit of God, as outlined in Romans 8, refer to himself as 'wretched', and utter the agonizing cry of despair: 'Who will deliver me?'

5. There is an apparent contradiction between the state of the 'wretched man' in Romans 7 and that of Paul in the rest of Scripture. The Paul of Romans 8 declared that 'Through Christ Jesus the law of the Spirit of life set me free from the law of sin and death' (8:2), and counts himself among those who 'do not walk according to the flesh but according to the Spirit' (8:4), who 'have the firstfruits of the Spirit' (8:23) and who experience the help of the Spirit in their weaknesses (8:26). But such assured confidences are totally missing from Romans 7.

6. In his other writings, Paul speaks confidently of his own standing in grace. To the Thessalonians he writes, 'You are witnesses, and so

is God, of how holy, righteous and blameless we were among you who believed' (1 Thess. 2:10). Indeed, Paul often proposes himself as a pattern to churches. 'Follow my example, as I follow the example of Christ,' he exhorts the Corinthians (1 Cor. 11:1). 'Whatever you have learned or received or heard from me, or seen in me — put it into practice. And the God of peace will be with you' (Phil. 4:9). He specifically rejected the accusations of those who considered him as walking according to the flesh (2 Cor. 1:17; 10:2).

7. Paul's confessions of frustration and defeat in Romans 7 seem totally at odds with statements he makes elsewhere concerning normative Christian experience. In 2 Corinthians 5:17 we read the glorious declaration: 'Therefore, if anyone is in Christ, he is a new creation, the old has gone, the new has come!' The change brought about by regeneration is profound indeed, and all-pervasive. In regenerate man sin is crucified. 'Those who belong to Christ Jesus have crucified the flesh with its passions and desires' (Gal. 5:24). They go on to put to death the misdeeds of the body (Rom. 8:12-14).

Assessment

Clearly this interpretation is supported by very strong arguments, The contrast between chapters 7 and 8 is indeed very marked, and it is not readily apparent how Paul in chapter 7 could speak so disparagingly about his life as a Christian. The cry of despair of one who confusedly considers life a condition of slavery to sin and a state of permanent warfare, from which he longs for deliverance, would appear to resemble more the state of the unconverted man in Adam than that of the Christian. These are very strong cumulative arguments in favour of this view.

Moreover, this interpretation accords very well with the cosmic redemptive-historical perspective of chapters 6 to 8 of Romans. The keynote of these chapters, and of what Paul there has to say about the life of the Christian and of the church, is his view of two antithetical world-orders. Chapters 7 and 8 form the climax of Paul's exposition of justification. The redemptive work of Christ on the cross is the breaking in of the new world, the kingdom of God. Christianity is not just a Jewish sect which believes that Jesus is the Messiah. The gospel is a message of divine power which introduces a new reign of grace. The subject of this whole section is entirely concerned with the work of salvation. The language of Romans 5 to 8 indicates clearly that we have to do with a problem of cosmic dimensions. Christ has liberated us from tyranny, and set us gloriously free through his redemptive victory. The subject of these chapters is the doctrine of redemption. This is presented in antithetical language. In order to display the glory of the triumph of the cross, Paul, as we have seen, presents it as victory over the tyrants of the old world-order — sin and death. But in chapter 7 he insists that freedom from the powers of sin and death takes concrete shape in freedom from the law. The law belongs to the old age of sin and death. The burden of Romans 7 is the powerlessness of the law in the struggle against sin, indeed its total inadequacy to vanquish the power of sin.

Käsemann presents this view when he writes, 'For Paul the antithesis of letter and Spirit is the same as flesh and Spirit. As he sees it, the presence of the risen Lord in the power of the Spirit takes the place of the Torah [law] of Moses and makes holy the world which otherwise, even in its piety and ethics, is unholy. The break with the law has to be proclaimed wherever the justification of the ungodly is the premise. This is just the point of the two chapters (7 and 8). On this is built both the discussion of the problem of unbelieving Israel in chapters 9 and 11 and the exhortation of chapters 12 to 13.'[1]

So in Romans 7 the elements placed over against each other are not (as in Galatians 5) the Spirit and the flesh, or (as in Romans 6) grace and the law, but the law of God and the law of sin. In the struggle between these parties the victory is to flesh and sin, for despite all that he wills and desires, the sinner finds himself in absolute bondage and in a situation of death. The whole contrast lies between the 'I myself' of verse 25 and the 'through Jesus Christ our Lord' of verse 24. The victory is none other than that of abandoning one's own dead works to embrace the righteousness of Christ; the motion is from sterile legalism, which only confirms the state of death, to the glorious liberty of those who through Christ enter the realm of the Spirit, and enjoy the victory described in chapter 8. Sinners, then, need to escape from the condemnation of chapter 7 into the experience of salvation of chapter 8.

Whatever else may be said about this way of considering chapter 7, it must be conceded that it accords perfectly with the biblical doctrine of justification by faith. This view not only protects the biblical gospel from attempts to impose upon it moralistic accretions or distortions; it presents with great strength and clarity the antithesis between any concept of salvation by works and salvation by sovereign grace. It also preserves the biblical doctrine of sanctification which grace upholds. The stark contrast between the experience of frustration and defeat of chapter 7 and that of victory and holiness in chapter 8 reflects the biblical note of victorious Christian living which grace ensures. However, while we may agree that this viewpoint harmonizes well with biblical doctrines, there are great difficulties which cause me to suggest that the arguments are not at all conclusive.

Difficulties

1. One point of weakness is most certainly the treatment accorded to the second part of 7:25. There, as we saw in our study of the text, after the triumphant conclusion in the first part of the verse that God has matched the wretchedness of our need by his full pardon for us in Christ, inexplicably that great climax affirming deliverance and victory lamely crumples into pathetic misery. 'Who will deliver me?' asks Paul. 'God will, through Christ,' came the confident reply. 'Thanks be to him!' And then, most unaccountably, follows the gloomy conclusion, which seems to smother the note of victory in an anguished cry of defeat: 'So then, I myself in my mind am a slave to God's law, but in the flesh a slave to the law of sin.'

So very difficult is it to reconcile this apparent anticlimax with the interpretation of Romans 7 which we have just outlined, that we find Moffatt in his translation of the New Testament taking the liberty of transferring the second part of verse 25 from its present position to follow the end of verse 23, arguing that this seems its original and logical position. But there is not a shred of textual evidence to justify such a rearrangement. Moffatt recognizes this fact and adds, 'We cannot avoid trusting our own judgement against the evidence.' This is a serious admission of unscholarly exegesis, and as J. I. Packer says, 'must cast doubt upon the theory which makes it necessary'.[2] Clearly a proper understanding of the passage has to do justice to its setting within the chapter, and no amount of wishful thinking will cause the second part of verse 25 to disappear.

It is part of the text, and has an important contribution to make to our understanding of the whole.

2. Another weighty argument against the understanding of Romans 7 as applying to the unregenerate man concerns the whole context of Romans in which the chapter is found. Throughout chapters 5 to 8 Paul is considering the meaning of the Christian life. He is describing what it means to have life in Christ. There is no indication in the text to support the idea that he suddenly digresses to consider man under law. Why should he suddenly turn away from his theme, in this the most logical of all his epistles, to consider the hopelessness of man's pre-Christian experience under the law?

In these four chapters Paul depicts the glorious freedom of the child of God. Through faith in Christ he has been freed from the dominion of the powers which prevailed over him in his pre-Christian state — wrath, sin, law and death. During the old Adamic age, he was under their tyranny. But in Christ all things have become new; he is now under grace, and under the dominion of life. He is saved from God's wrath through Christ's death and resurrection (5:9), rescued from the dominion of sin through union with Christ (6:5-14), liberated from the authority of law through the death of Christ (7:4) and from condemnation of death through the victory of Christ (8:2).

The Christian has been rescued from these great prevailing powers of the old Adamic realm, and now belongs to the realm of life. But as yet he lives upon this earth, in a still imperfect state. He belongs to the new age, but still lives in the flesh. Hence the tension and cry for deliverance. His dilemma is caused by his double status, in the world, yet not of it, The dualism is not that of a divided soul, torn in two directions, but a heart united in its delight in God and yet dissatisfied because of its double situation.

The old way of the written code no longer holds us in bondage, for we have been released from the law; now we serve in the way of the Spirit (7:6). And just as law-righteousness was powerless to justify the sinner (7:7-13), it is equally powerless to sanctify the believer (7:14-25).

I believe that this is the natural way to understand the passage in its context. In this whole section the apostle expresses not an apprehension of wrath for unpardoned sin, but a sense of self-loathing on account of indwelling corruption. The whole context is a very strong pointer towards the accuracy of the Reformed view.

3. A third argument concerns the change of tenses in chapter 7. Throughout the first thirteen verses Paul speaks of himself consistently in the past tense, whereas in verses 14-25 he changes to the present tense. That change is signalled in verses 5 and 6 where, having spoken of what we once were (7:5), he proceeds to speak of what we henceforth are as Christians. He then goes on to develop that contrast in the verses which follow. The natural way to understand verses 14-25, then, is to see them as descriptive of the present life of the believer. Only by ignoring what the text actually says is it possible to construct the paragraph differently. While it is granted that sometimes in the Gospel narratives the evangelists, especially Mark, for the sake of vividness, describe what is clearly a past event using a present tense, there is no clear example of Paul doing this in any of his writings. Besides, this passage is not a piece of narrative writing. We have no grounds for ignoring the actual words and tenses used in the text.

4. There is nothing stated in this passage which contradicts what Paul states elsewhere of the experience of a believer. The conflict which is depicted is entirely compatible with an experience of regeneration.

This section of Romans 7 most definitely does not describe a man whose spiritual existence is split, with two clashing wills dwelling in his breast, a desire for the good existing side by side with a desire for the evil. There is not the slightest hint that the man of Romans 7 has a desire for the evil. He hates it. His will is united in desiring the good. There is no dualism in his aspiration and will. What Paul laments is not that the will simultaneously desires something else, but that the will does not achieve all it desires. Only if the will is united in seeking good can the writer say that he delights in the law of God.

Such expressions of frustration and regret are not inconsistent with a work of grace in the heart. Who dare say that the Christian life is one long sequence of undisturbed serenity and perpetual victory? As Nygren points out, in chapter 8:23 ('We groan inwardly'), out of the very midst of the chapter of triumphant faith comes an expression reflecting a measure of dissatisfaction with the incompleteness of the level of attainment. 'It is not only in the outer life of the Christian that weakness grips him. It is a tragic reality in his inner life, in his life with God, in his very prayer life.'[3]

How careful Paul is in writing to the Philippians to confess that he does not consider himself to have attained! (Phil. 3:8). And to the Corinthians he confesses the existence of a certain fearfulness mingled with his faith, for his heart still trembles lest he who has preached to others should himself 'become a castaway'.

There is a certain duality in the life of a Christian, but it is not duality of will. There is tension between the believer's intention and his performance, for no matter now mature he may be, 'his reach will always exceed his grasp'. Indeed the more he progresses along the pathway of holiness, the greater will be his feeling of frustration at the chasm between his awareness of the corruption of his nature and his longing for glory.

This state of permanent lack of perfect achievement in the moral life, which is described in Romans 7, is an inevitable part of Christian experience. The dualism, as I have attempted to show in my exposition of the text, is the Christian's double situation as someone living in the present age and yet in a very real sense belonging to the age to come, and dwelling in heavenly places in Christ Jesus. Tension and frustration there must be, calling for eternal vigilance and constant longing. He has the will to do good, but sin is present with him. With his heart he serves the law of God, but he still lives in the flesh.

The very same dualism faces us in both chapters 6 and 8. In chapter 6 we are free from sin, yet must do battle against it. In chapter 7 we are free from the law, yet we are not righteous according to its spiritual standards. In chapter 8 we are free from death, yet we long for the redemption of our bodies.

As long as life lasts, the tension between the old and the new, between the heart and the members, will continue. As long as he lives 'in the flesh', that is in a body, on this physical earth, the Christian is in the body of death, and experiences the tension between being 'in Christ' and being 'in the flesh'. It is therefore entirely natural that he should yearn to be freed from the body of death, and long for the time when the perishable puts on the imperishable and the mortal puts on immortality (1 Cor. 15).

Paul's cry is not a cry of despair, for he goes on immediately to express thanksgiving: 'Thanks be to God — through Jesus Christ our Lord!' Through the victory already accomplished by Christ, he can look forward to the day of full and final redemption.

5. Various expressions found in chapter 7 are compatible with what Paul says elsewhere of the believer's experience. In Philippians 3:6, speaking of his life as a Pharisee, he states that as to righteousness under the law, he had considered himself blameless. That is to say that, as a zealous Pharisee, prior to his conversion to Christianity, before he experienced the regenerating work of the Holy Spirit in his life, he was found blameless. That was the verdict of the self-righteous sinner: no sense of sin or need, no expression of remorse or repentance, nothing but self-satisfaction and complacency! How different is his position as depicted in Romans 7, where as a child of God he laments the remnants of sin in his life! Other similar expressions of note are 'In my inner being I delight in God's law', and 'I myself in my mind am a slave to God's law.'

6. We note the view of Dr Martyn Lloyd-Jones, who applies the passage to an unregenerate person who is experiencing intense conviction of sin. Dr Lloyd-Jones is undoubtedly absolutely correct in stating that Paul's purpose and intention was not strictly to write a piece of autobiography. His concern was the law of God, its function and its limitations. But it seems to me that the whole setting of the chapter in Romans, and the particular paragraph in its context in chapter 7, shows that Paul was demonstrating the law's inability not just to justify the sinner, but to sanctify the saint.

The point I want to make here, however, is that a proper understanding of the passage must account for its intensely personal note. Dr Lloyd-Jones maintains that in this section the apostle is not primarily writing about himself or his own experience, but is depicting graphically a man who is experiencing intense conviction of sin. He feels totally condemned, but has not yet come to understand the truth of the gospel.

In my estimation, this view has the advantage over other presentations of the unregenerate position in that it explains the cause of the complaint: the Holy Spirit has awakened the sinner to his lost condition, and caused him to feel intensely his sinfulness and deep need. Nevertheless, it too fails to account for the intensely personal note of this passage.

There is every indication that even as he wrote, Paul felt deeply the reality of what he was describing. There is nothing theatrical here. This is not simply reminiscence of the experiences of a distant past. Nor is it merely a theological statement of general application portrayed in passionate personal terms. This was Paul's experience as he wrote these lines. To suggest that it describes a person under intense personal conviction of sin, feeling utterly condemned before the spirituality of the law, is to represent the apostle as writing in the first person singular for merely literary reasons, to render the experience more intense and graphic. But according to the view of Dr Lloyd-Jones, this is not Paul's experience at the time of writing, and must be adjudged just a literary device to render the dilemma more vivid. This seems not just unusual, but totally foreign to the overriding purpose of Paul, and to the transparent sincerity of the passage. There is a ring of personal emotion that the apostle honestly feels even as he writes. He experiences the intensity of the struggle as he writes the lines. 'The passage is not a mere abstract, but was written in Paul's very heart blood and bears all the evidence of having been wrung from the agony of his soul. We sense the throb of a personal pain pulsating through its every word.'[4] We must account for the change of tense, from past to present, and the personal agony expressed, in a way which Dr Lloyd-Jones' theory does not.

Nor does his theory account for the concluding statement in verse 25, coming immediately after the triumphant assertion of the early part of the verse. This can be nothing but the writer's concluding assessment of his present condition, depicting the believer's continuing struggle with the remnants of sin.

7. Sufficient attention is not given by proponents of the unregenerate view to the fact that the longing expressed in the passage is for deliverance 'out of the body of this death', a theme which, as we have seen, is taken up and expanded so appropriately in 8:23. There the apostle, again writing of his own desires, but now associating himself with other believers, writes, 'We ourselves, who have the first-fruits of the Spirit, groan inwardly as we wait eagerly for our adoption as sons, the redemption of our bodies.' In chapter 7:14-25, as in the opening verses of chapter 8, Paul is not speaking of justification, nor of the fact of there now being 'no condemnation for those who are in Christ Jesus' in a forensic sense, as acquittal from guilt, but freedom through the Spirit from the tyranny and power of sin as a dominating force. The prospect in which he rejoices is that of the perfect fulfilment of our aspirations

and hopes of full and final deliverance from the realm of sin when comes the consummation of Christ's work of redemption, the redemption of our bodies.

Conclusion

It is my opinion that the cumulative weight of these seven objections to the unregenerate understanding of the passage makes this position untenable. For a more compelling and consistent exegesis of the verses I would recommend the commentaries by John Murray, Ernest Kevan, J. I. Packer, Anders Nygren, R. Haldane, Charles Hodge, C. E. B. Cranfield, Leon Morris, F. F. Bruce, Matthew Henry, Louis Berkhof, G. B. Wilson, John Owen, James Fraser and the unanimous voice of the Puritans.

Appendix II:
The unsanctified Christian

The first position we considered had no direct bearing on the doctrine of sanctification, since it viewed the 'wretched man' of Romans 7:14-25 as an unregenerate person, a stranger to grace and to God. This cannot be said of the second position which we must now consider. According to this view, often termed the 'higher-life' system of sanctification, the person in question in this passage is regenerate, but is wholly dissatisfied with his life. Though a Christian, he knows only heartbreaking defeat, ineffectual struggle and spiritual stalemate. It is the description of a defeated, 'carnal' Christian, wholly frustrated, longing for deliverance.

We have already noted the importance of Wesley in sowing the seeds of a doctrine of Perfectionism which was to produce a crop of movements teaching the 'higher-life' theory of sanctification.

B. B. Warfield writes, 'We attribute to Wesley's impulse the wide prevalence in our modern Protestantism of what has come to be known as "holiness teaching". As move after move of the "holiness movement" has broken over us during the last century, each has brought, no doubt, something distinctive of itself. But a common fundamental character has informed them all, and this common fundamental character has been communicated to them by the Wesleyan doctrine. The essential elements of that doctrine repeat themselves in all these movements, and form their characteristic features.'[1]

This theory of sanctification comes under a number of names and titles, among which are — the victorious life, the higher Christian life, Christian perfection, entire sanctification, sanctification by faith, full gospel holiness, the release of the Spirit, scriptural brokenness and total abandonment. It came to be identified with various historic movements such as the Fellowship Movement, the Sanctification Movement, English Methodism, the Victorious Life Movement, the Keswick Convention and Pentecostalism, and has affected much of the modern charismatic movement.

Basically the higher-life movement arose as a reaction against the Reformed doctrine of sanctification which seemed to console the pious for their sins. In 1952 Dr Steven Barnabas in his book *So Great Salvation,* which represented the distinctive and characteristic view of the Keswick teaching at that time, states that a threefold charge has been levelled against the Reformed doctrine of salvation: firstly, that the average Christian altogether ignores the biblical demand that sanctification should accompany justification, and so by his unholy life divides two things which God has joined; secondly, that most of those few who pursue holiness fail to attain it, through seeking it in a spirit of Pelagian self-reliance by a regimen of self-effort; and thirdly, that all alike hold an inadequate view of what the Holy Spirit was sent to do in the lives of the people of God.

A characteristic of such theories is the view that sanctification is effected through a crisis experience. It is primarily neither an achievement nor a process, but a gift. For some this crisis experience is described as the 'baptism of, or in, the Holy Spirit', while others term it a 'second blessing', or an experience of 'entire sanctification', or the 'fulness of the Spirit'. The view generally is that sanctification begins with regeneration, in the sense that the Holy Spirit takes up his abode in the believer, and from that time on does as much in the believer's life as he is permitted to do. Sanctification in real earnest begins with a crisis. Man's will controls and therefore stands apart from the Spirit's sanctifying action. Hence, through this distinct and separate work of the Spirit, this gift of sanctification, the sanctified believer moves from an experience of struggle and defeat into one of constant victory.

It was John Wesley who infected the modern Protestant world with this notion of entire instantaneous sanctification, though he himself never claimed perfection. To support his position he distinguished sharply between justification and sanctification, alleging that they were produced through separate acts of faith. This meant that there are two types of Christians — those who are only justified and those who are also sanctified.

Charles Finney embraced this view, and expressed it forcibly and clearly: 'Full faith in the word and promise of God naturally, and certainly and immediately produces a state of entire sanctification... This result is instantaneous on the exercise of faith, and in this sense sanctification is an instantaneous work. The sense in which I use the term entire sanctification includes all that is implied in perfect obedience to the law of God.[2]

This sharp distinction between justification and sanctification is a keynote of the Perfectionist movement. So too is the emphasis on immediate sanctification, received by faith, as a distinct and separate gift. The precise vocabulary varies from movement to movement, but all emphasize the note of victory in the New Testament writing, the power of the Holy Spirit, and the inadequacy of regeneration to ensure normative Christian experience. It is held to be necessary to move from one level of Christian experience, secured by justification, to a higher level, secured by instantaneous sanctification.

Because of the characteristic doctrines of the higher-life movement, they consistently reject the Reformed or regenerate view of Romans 7. Dr Steven Barnabas, for example, representing one of the most moderate branches of the higher-life teaching, that of the Keswick Convention movement, rejects the Reformed view that Romans 7 reflects Paul's normal everyday experience, on the grounds that it records only 'heartbreaking defeat', 'ineffectual struggle', and 'spiritual stalemate'.[3] This Barnabas affirms, rightly, is not the New Testament picture of healthy Christian life. 'The *normal* Christian life', he continues, 'is one of uniform sustained victory over sin... A life of victory over conscious sin is the rightful heritage of every child of God... By the constant surrender of his will to the Holy Spirit he [the Christian] finds a power in God that *completely* conquers the flesh and brings deliverance from its lusts.' Anything less than complete victory for such people is considered defeat. And defeat need never be: 'The privilege of the believer is this, that he may so live in the Spirit that, speaking from consciousness, he may be tempted to say the flesh no longer exists.' Dr Barnabas quotes with approval the remark that 'If normal Christian experience does not rise any higher than that, then we must change our Lord's invitation to read, "Come unto me all ye that labour and are heavy-laden, and I will tell you how to be wretched!"' Instead, he affirms that verses 7-25 of Romans 7 show 'what happens when any person, regenerate or unregenerate, tries to conquer the old nature by self-effort', that is, without the use of the Keswick technique of consecration and faith. 'The key to the interpretation,' it is suggested, 'is found in the frequent use of "I", while there is not a single mention of the Holy Spirit. In chapter 8, however, where there are at least twenty references to the Holy Spirit, and the "I" drops out, there is a triumphant note throughout...' Normal Christian living, therefore, is not to be found in Romans 7 but in Romans 8, '...and is experienced as the Holy Spirit by his counteractive power is permitted to have his way'.

According to those who hold this view, then, Romans 7 is a description of the experience of a carnal, unsanctified Christian and a statement of how through an additional work of the Holy Spirit we obtain sanctification. We must at all costs get out of chapter 7 into chapter 8. Romans 7 is not to be the normal Christian experience. It tells us to get out of the defeat, misery and agony of chapter 7 and come into the victory of chapter 8. We must cross over the Jordan into the promised land of chapter 8. We must leave behind the wandering and agony of chapter 7 and come into the higher experience of chapter 8. Triumphalism, not defeatism, is New Testament Christianity. We must yield to God, in full surrender, and receive by faith the gift of sanctification. 'Let go and let God!' is their cry. There is a double condition of sanctification, surrender and faith.

We are happy to note that many over recent years who are associated with the Keswick movement neither hold nor preach such a doctrine of instant sanctification; but in so far as Dr Barnabas' book was the official presentation of the Keswick doctrine when it appeared, it illustrates the view which historically prevailed.

A modified form of this view has been presented by Dr C. L. Mitton. He rejects the idea that Romans 7 can be interpreted either as describing Paul's pre-Christian experience or his mature Christian experience, and posits a third possibility which appears to him to incorporate the merits of the other two, while avoiding their weaknesses. He argues that the chapter is a description both of 'the miserable past' from which the Christian has been delivered, and also 'the miserable present' into which he may fall again, if ever he begins to imagine that it is in his own strength that he stands. He quotes with approval A. E. Garvie. Even in the Christian, 'Holiness will sometimes cease to be for him the spontaneous exercise of an indwelling power, and will appear as a hard task to be discharged; the contrast between desire and duty ... will present itself in his experience though Christian... This experience is not his as a Christian, but in so far as he falls short of claiming and using the grace offered him in Christ.'[4]

Mitton largely builds his interpretation on the second part of verse 25, which is the very point where the problem appears most intractable. 'So then I myself with the mind serve the law of God, but with the flesh the law of sin.' He insists that interpreters do not give sufficient weight to the phrase translated 'I myself', and that they consider the contrast between 'mind' and 'flesh' sufficient to convey the sense of the verse. Mitton holds that the phrase in question is exceedingly emphatic, and of great importance. He translates it as 'I left to myself', or 'I in my own nature', or, 'I entirely on my own'. He writes, 'The significance of these pronouns seems to make it clear that Paul is here speaking of himself as he is "entirely on his own", without that inward reinforcement and cleansing associated with a true conversion. It is not a question at all of whether this is past or present. It is a question of the difference between the man who is "entirely on his own" in his effort to achieve righteousness, and the man who is "in Christ", and who is therefore fortified by the Holy Spirit. It is the mark of the sad plight of our human nature that even after we have been delivered from that moral isolation from God, which inevitably spells defeat, we can still slip back into it, and experience all over again its characteristic helplessness and frustration.

'On this interpretation Romans 7:14-25 becomes a description of the distressing experience of any morally earnest man, whether Christian or not, who attempts to live up to the commands of God "on his own", without that constant reliance upon the uninterrupted supply of the resources of God, which is characteristic of the mature Christian... It can also be true of the converted Christian who has slipped back, as can so easily happen, from daily dependence upon the grace of God in Christ into a legalistic attitude to God and to righteousness. So it is both past and present in its reference, since Paul looks back to the time before Christ transformed his life, and came to "live in" him, when he was "on his own", and also humbly recognizes that pride and carelessness may bring him back again into what ought to lie wholly in the past, but may return into the present.'[5]

Mitton argues that his interpretation explains the use of the present tense throughout verses 14-25. If Paul is thought to be describing not merely a past experience, but one which is potentially ever present, then the use of the present is logical.

Mitton describes the normal Christian as a 'moral diabetic', whose experience is similar to that of a 'controlled diabetic', able to live a normal life through the regular use of doses of insulin. 'So man, the moral diabetic, may receive into his ailing nature Divine reinforcement, which establishes a "control" over his sinful nature. Let him however, at any time, cease to avail himself of the constantly offered gift of the Holy Spirit, which is the privilege of all who are "in Christ", and his ailment reasserts itself, and his borrowed life is forfeit. He is never wholly cured, no matter how fit and well he seems to be by virtue of his vicarious health. His illness is only controlled and it remains so long as the controlling power is regularly received.'[6]

All the above views share the notion that Romans 7 is not the description of normative Christian experience, and is in stark contrast to chapter 8. While Mitton is more guarded in that he does not offer a specific technique of sanctification to translate the Christian from chapter 7 to chapter 8, nevertheless he too maintains that chapter 7 depicts an abnormal and unspiritual state from which we must seek deliverance through the Spirit. Once again we must endeavour to get out of chapter 7 into chapter 8. To do so is to experience sanctification.

Assessment

At first glance there is much in the higher-life theory of sanctification which seems to fit the context of Romans 7:14-25.

1. Firstly, their rejection of 'miserable-sinner' Christianity in favour of a work of the Holy Spirit, in which a person is translated from an experience of frustration and defeat into an experience of victory is entirely in accordance with what Scripture teaches about definitive sanctification. When we speak of sanctification we usually have in mind that process of spiritual transformation by which the believer, through the action of the Holy Spirit,

increasingly is enabled to die to sin and to live unto righteousness. This notion, of course, is entirely biblical. But often the Scriptures speak of sanctification as definitive. Like our regeneration, justification and adoption, sanctification is an act of God effected once for all. Paul, for example, addresses believers at Corinth, with all their moral imperfections, as the church of God, 'sanctified in Christ Jesus and called to be saints' (1 Cor. 1:2), and later in the same epistle reminds them that they were washed, sanctified and justified (1 Cor. 6:11).

John Murray writes, 'We are thus compelled to take account of the fact that the language of sanctification is used with reference to the same decisive action that occurs at the inception of the Christian life, and one that characterizes the people of God in their identity as called effectually by God's grace. It would be, therefore, a deflection from biblical patterns of language and conception to think of sanctification exclusively in terms of a progressive work.'[7]

R. B. Gaffin expresses the same truth when he writes, 'It is important to note that, although the apostle [Paul] is certainly concerned with the progressive transformation in thought, desire and conduct which the believer must undergo, and the reality of his continuing struggle with sin (Rom. 7:14-25; Gal. 5:13-26), still the vocabulary of sanctification which he employs has reference characteristically not to a process but to a definitive act which occurs at the inception of the life of faith.'[8]

Both Murray and Gaffin refer to Romans chapter 6 as a passage which is crucial for a proper understanding of the definitive nature of sanctification. The antithesis between death and life highlights the decisive breach which the resurrection of Christ and the regeneration of the believer involve, our solidarity with Christ ensuring the latter on the basis of the former. Sanctification is the eschatological deliverance from one age or world-order, and the entrance into the new age.

It is clear, then, that justification, adoption, sanctification and glorification, as applied to the Christian, are not separate distinct acts, but rather each describes a different facet or aspect of the one act of being raised.

Murray, commenting on Romans 6:10, 'For in that he died, he died unto sin once,' draws attention to this once-for-allness that is Paul's paramount interest in this part of the epistle. He argues, in my view convincingly, that it is to the power of sin that Christ died, and that by his resurrection he triumphed over the power of sin, thereby ensuring victory over sin for those united to him.

'Christ was identified in such a way with the sin which he vicariously bore that he dealt not only with its guilt but also with its power. Death ruled over him until he broke its power (v.9). So sin may be said to have ruled over him in that his humiliation state was conditioned by the sin with which he was vicariously identified. He was made sin (2 Cor. 5:21) and sin as power must be taken into account in this relationship. It was by his own dying that he destroyed the power of sin, and in his resurrection he entered upon a state that was not conditioned by sin. There is good reason to believe that it is this victory over sin as power that the apostle has in view when he says that Christ "died to sin once". And it is because Christ triumphed over the power of sin in his death that those united to him in his death die to the power of sin and become dead to sin (vv.2,11)'.[9]

It is the consistent teaching of the New Testament that sin is dethroned in every person who is effectually called, united to Christ and regenerated. Calling unites us to Christ (1 Cor. 1:9) and if the person called is united to Christ, he is united to him in the virtue of his death and the power of his resurrection: he is dead to sin; the old man, the old unregenerate self, has been destroyed, sin no longer exercises dominion over him. 'Sin shall not have dominion over you, for you are not under law but under grace' (Rom. 6:14, NKJV). This is not an exhortation but a plain statement of fact. Sin will not have dominion over the person who is under grace. The exhortations in the passage are based on that fact. Those in Christ are to reckon themselves, that is, to consider themselves, 'dead indeed unto sin, but alive unto God'. Through the death and resurrection of Christ the believer is dead to the rule, reign and dominion of sin, and is definitively sanctified. This is the consistent teaching of the New Testament.

2. Perfectionists are right when they claim that this freedom from the dominion of sin, this victory over the power of sin, is not achieved by process, nor by our striving or working to that end; they are entirely right when they insist that it is a momentary act realized by faith.

However, while Perfectionists are right in these two aspects, it seems to me that they make five radical mistakes which distort their whole construction of the doctrine of sanctification.

Firstly, they fail to recognize that this victory is the possession of everyone who is regenerate and effectually called. There is a transcendent finality in the work of Christ. Every Christian has been crucified with Christ. He is united to Christ in his death and resurrection. He is not *dying* unto sin, but *dead* to it. This is true of every believer. Christ has crucified his fallen nature. The Christian is not to seek a crisis experience of crucifixion. He is to take stock ('reckon', Rom. 6:11) of what he possesses. The process is not *to* death as the end, but *from* death as a beginning to mortification of what Christ has slain. The movement is from inward fact, through working faith, to outward and glorious reality. This is the biblical doctrine of sanctification. In Christ we are dead to sin but alive to God. We are exhorted, then, to mortify our members, and to live out this victory which God has gloriously wrought for us in Christ, and in us by his Spirit.

Secondly, Perfectionists construe the victory as a blessing separable from the state of justification, thereby attempting to rend asunder two things which God has irreversibly joined together. A. A. Hodge speaks of this indissoluble union thus: 'You cannot take Christ for justification unless you take him for sanctification. You can no more separate the circulation of the blood from the inhalation of the air. Breathing and circulation are two different things, but you cannot have the one without the other; they go together and they constitute one life.'[10]

Thirdly, they represent the Christian victory as something very different from what the Scriptures represent it to be. They portray it as freedom from sinning, or freedom from conscious sin. The Scriptures teach that the victory entailed in our sanctification is the radical breach with *the power and love of sin* which is necessarily the possession of everyone who has been united to Christ. Union with Christ is union with him in the efficacy of his death and in the virtue of his resurrection; he who thus died and rose again with Christ is freed from sin, and sin will not exercise dominion over him.

Fourthly, they totally underestimate and misrepresent the biblical teaching of regeneration. The Holy Spirit is the controlling and directing agent in every regenerate person. For this reason the fundamental principle, the governing disposition, the prevailing character of every regenerate person is holiness. He is 'spiritual', and he delights in the law of God in his inner being (Rom. 7:22; 1 Cor. 2:14-15). Everyone effectually called by God and regenerated by the Spirit has secured the victory in terms of Romans 6:14; 1 John 3:9; 5:4,18. As John Murray states so well, 'This victory is actual or it is nothing. It is a reflection upon and a deflection from the pervasive New Testament witness to speak of it as merely potential or positional.'[11]

Fifthly, their division of Christians into two classes, spiritual (or sanctified) and carnal (unsanctified) undermines the biblical doctrine of regeneration and definitive sanctification. While a superficial reading of Romans 7 would seem to support such a view, particularly verses 14 and 25, where Paul speaks of being 'carnal' and 'a slave to the law of sin', we have seen in our exegesis of these verses that they cannot be used to support the idea of a two-tier system of sanctification. When Paul speaks of classes, he knows of only two, as is clear from 1 Corinthians 2, where he divides men into 'natural' and 'spiritual'. Similarly in Romans 8, the division he again makes is that of the Christian and the non-Christian, for example, in verses 8 and 9 where the contrast is between those who are controlled by the flesh and those who, because God lives in them, are controlled by the Spirit. There is no question of a third group, composed of unspiritual Christians. The two terms are mutually exclusive.

The various presentations of the higher-life theory of sanctification, whether in one of its more extreme forms, or, as with Mitton, in a more modified form, all present a truncated theology of sanctification which basically is at variance with the Reformed biblical doctrine of sanctification. Warfield recognizes the nature of this reaction, and identifies it as a revolt against the whole doctrine of grace: 'The perfectionist teaching of these several movements, whether in its crasser or in its more guarded forms, is a revolt against the Reformation doctrine not only of the continued imperfection of the Christian in this life where he enjoys only the first-fruits of salvation, but of sin and grace in general, which constitutes the pivot on which the whole system of Reformation teaching turns... The most striking thing about the long-continued attempt which has been made to prove that Paul the Christian was a sinless man is the clearness with which it has come out that Paul knew nothing of a sinless man in this life.'[12]

We must similarly reject Mitton's 'moral diabetic' doctrine of sanctification as a spineless doctrine which eviscerates Christianity of its great doctrines of grace that produce holiness, rather than ailment and emasculation. We are reminded of the statement made by Dr F. L. Patton, President of Princeton Seminary, concerning what he called the 'New Christianity' which 'appears as a disease and as an epidemic'. Referring to the historic Reformed faith he commented, 'I rejoice that it is a system so co-ordinated, whose doctrines are so concatenated, which has been so logically constructed, that if discovered in some future age by an excavating palaeontologist he would be forced to remark: "Gentlemen, this belonged to the order of vertebrates!"'[13]

We have seen in our study of the text that Mitton's theory is based on a strained construction of the phrase 'I myself'. Certainly the 'controlled diabetic' theory is difficult to reconcile with the theme of triumphant resurrection of chapter 6, and that of life through the Spirit of chapter 8. The theory underestimates the biblical doctrine of regeneration, and its consequences for sanctification and glorification. There is no such thing as an unsanctified Christian.

Appendix III
Barth and the modern liberal approach

As we have seen, Barth's approach is very different from that of others who understand the man of Romans 7 in terms of regeneration or unregeneration, sanctification or unsanctification. These traditional categories are abandoned for a philosophical approach to religion and faith. Barth was above all a dialectic philosopher, and his inclination towards dialectics predominates over everything else.

He declares that man, every man, Christian and non-Christian alike, lives in a state of 'contradiction'. Religion offers no solution to vital questions concerning man's existence. Through religion man becomes a deeper and more inscrutable enigma than before. There is no deliverance or liberty through religion, only the discovery of non-deliverance.

If the question is asked whether the contradiction of the religious man in Romans 7 is past, one must answer that in a certain sense this is so since in Christ the Christian is dead to the law of sin and death, and is delivered from this contradiction. Nevertheless, according to verse 24, contradiction is still the lot of the Christian. The deliverance has not taken place in his person or experience, but in the person of Jesus Christ. Thus Paul is two men at the same time, the man who asks the question, the miserable man, and yet the man of the response to the question. In his present experience the past is still present. The reality of his life is contradiction.

But Jesus Christ is the new man, the man who has passed from death to life, the man that in myself I am not and can never be. Jesus Christ is what I am not: he is my existential 'I', the 'I' that I am in

God, in the liberty of God. The solution to man's contradiction is thus found in the existential decision of faith. Thus Barth in his commentary on Romans maintains that in chapter 7 Paul depicts the situation of our own past which has been surpassed by faith.

It would be totally inaccurate to consider Barth as speaking of the man in Romans 7 as a believer. For Barth it is not a question of historical categories, before or after conversion. His sole consideration is that of existential categories. The one and the same man depicted in the chapter — religious, but outside of Christ; or Christian, united to Christ — continues ever to be a man in contradiction, entirely sinner and entirely sanctified. Thus the duality in man is not historic or personal, but existential.

Barth argues that the 'religious decision' of God passes upon all men through Christ, just as the condemnation passed upon all through Adam. The first relationship is primary. 'Man's essential and original nature is to be found, therefore, not in Adam but in Christ.' [1] The implication of this is universalism, not just in respect of atonement, but also of justification. That is to say that Christ died for all men, and justifies all men. The reign of grace through righteousness unto eternal life must embrace all men without exception. Thus Karl Barth makes the justification of sinners into the passing of a verdict which is totally without any element of reality. Human life is lived out between these two poles, God's judgement and his grace, but does not in any real sense affect him nor change him.

This modern liberal approach, which is epitomized by the Barthian approach, is less concerned with categories of personal experience, such as sanctification, than with a supra-personal *Heilgeschichte,* or history of salvation. Here historic Christianity is virtually reduced to monistic process philosophy. Ethics is identical with a process of election. The Christ of Barth is not the Christ of the historic Christian creeds. He stands for the process of interaction between God and man. Barth speaks of interpreting ethics theologically. For him there is no God apart from Christ, as there is no man apart from Christ. In Christ the commanding God and obedient man have coalesced. There was no *creatio ex nihilo.* There was no historical Adam. God did not reveal himself directly in nature and history. The virgin birth, the death and the resurrection of Christ did not take place in history but in super-history. And super-history is not measured in hours and days of ordinary history.

There is no difference of date between the first and the second coming of Christ. There is no difference of date between what Christ did, or rather *does* for us, and what he, through the Spirit, does within us. In Christ God has time for us; in Christ he is buried with us, with all men. In Christ our time becomes God's time; we, all men, are risen with him. All revelation events are aspects of the one great resurrection event, of which God and man are the two correlative aspects.

The implication of Barth's theology is universalism, not just in respect of atonement and justification, but also of sanctification. This being so, and in view of the limited nature of our study, we shall not engage in any detailed examination or rebuttal of such views. I consider, however, that Barth's theology is more christocentric than the Bible, and, despite his own polemic against natural theology, that he erected a theology that was in many ways speculative, on the basis of a biblical core.

I esteem the judgement of Van Til to be correct when he concludes that 'The gospel of Barth is an emasculated gospel, a gospel without God, without Christ, without grace, a gospel to the liking of the natural man and withal a gospel of despair.'[2] The monistic universalistic philosophical presuppositions of Barth do not help us in our attempt to understand the significance of the doctrine of sanctification as taught in Romans.

For further reading

It will be clear that for the interpretation of Romans 7 set forth in this book, I am indebted to a host of commentators whose contribution to the study of the passage has been invaluable. Apart from the detailed references found at the end of this book, mention should be made of some writers whose work has been particularly helpful, and which I warmly recommend for further study.

My own interest in the epistle to the Romans was greatly stimulated by the preaching and writings of *Dr D. Martyn Lloyd-Jones*. While it has been argued earlier that Dr Lloyd-Jones was mistaken in his interpretation of the latter part of Romans 7, his commentaries on Romans are of immense value, and will greatly reward careful reading. His exposition of chapter 6, entitled *The New Man*, is thrilling, particularly his exposure of false higher-life notions of sanctification, and his clinical analysis of Paul's statements regarding the nature of the believer's standing through Christ. His commentary on chapter 8 is glorious indeed. If I feel obliged to disagree with Dr Lloyd-Jones in his interpretation of Romans 7, in all other respects his commentaries on this epistle are totally in the mould of Reformed preaching at its best, and are heartily recommended. They are published by the Banner of Truth Trust.

Another thoroughly satisfying commentary on Romans is that of *Professor John Murray*, published in the New International Commentary series by Marshall Morgan and Scott. Here we find scholarly exegesis of the highest order, and his interpretation of Romans 7 is thoroughly satisfying. In addition to this major work, I warmly recommend his article entitled 'Sanctification' in the *Bulletin of the Evangelical Library* (No. 13, Autumn 1953).

For an understanding of the structure of the epistle, and of the logical development of the apostle's thought, I can recommend *Anders Nygren's Commentary on Romans*, published by Fortress Press, Philadelphia. It is very readable, and while it lacks John Murray's penetrating spiritual perception regarding the saint's sanctification, it is very helpful in its overall analysis. (John Murray's review of this commentary is found in his *Collected writings,* vol.3, pp. 350-55.)

A most rewarding study of the subject is that entitled *A Treatise on Sanctification* by *James Fraser* of Alness, an eighteenth-century Scottish divine. It is a work of major importance, detailed in its exegesis and richly spiritual in its application. It is an exposition of Romans chapters 6, 7 and 8:1-4, and is described by Murray as 'one of the ablest and most thorough treatments of the question and of the considerations in support of the view that Paul is describing his experience in a state of grace'. It has just been republished by Old Paths Publications.

Other commentaries not to be ignored are those of *John Calvin, Charles Hodge* and *Robert Haldane,* all of whom expound Romans 7:14-25 as referring to the believer.

Two scholarly articles by *E. F. Kevan,* in which he deals with chapters 7 and 8 of Romans are most helpful. They are entitled 'The Saving Work of the Holy Spirit', and appear in *The Keswick Week,* London, 1953.

I can heartily recommend two excellent articles by *Dr J. I. Packer.* The first, entitled 'The Wretched Man in Romans 7', is found in *Studia Evangelica II* (41). The second, 'Keswick and the Reformed Doctrine of Sanctification' (*Evangelical Quarterly,* July 1955) is of particular interest in that it is thoroughly documented from Keswick sources.

Peter Masters and *Paul Brown* have produced a very thought-provoking study entitled *Which System of Sanctification?* in which they contrast higher-life systems with the biblical doctrine of sanctification. It is published by the Metropolitan Tabernacle and is a worthy contribution to the discussion.

Finally, I must draw attention to the 1955 annual lecture of the Evangelical Library by *Edwin Lewis* entitled, *The Puritans and the Seventh of Romans.* In this interesting historical survey, the works of men like Owen, Goodwin and Charnock are examined with reference to sanctification, mortification of sin and Romans 7.

References

Chapter 1

1. Quoted by C. L. Mitton, 'Romans 7 Reconsidered,' three articles in the *Expository Times*, no. 65, pp.78-80, 99-103, 132-5. This quotation comes on p.79.
2. Kümmel, *Römer 7 und die Bekehrung des Paulus*.
3. P. Althaus, 'Der Brief an die Römer,' in *Das Neue Testament Deutsch*, vol. 6, 1932, Vandenhoeck & Ruprecht.
4. H. Ridderbos, *Paul: an Outline of his Theology*, Eerdmans, 1975.
5. R. Bultmann, *Römer 7 und die Anthropologie des Paulus*.
6. E. Käsemann, 'An die Römer,' in *Handbuch zum Neuen Testament*, B. Mohr, 1973.
7. D. M. Lloyd-Jones, *Romans vol. 6: The Law — its Function and its Limits*, Banner of Truth, 1973.
8. As above, pp.256-7.
9. Augustine, *Retractions*, 81, ch.23.
10. J. Calvin, *Commentary on Romans*, Seeley, 1934, p.286.
11. Mitton, 'Romans 7 Reconsidered,' p.78
12. J. Wesley, quoted by Mitton, as above.
13. J. M. F. Cruvellier, *L'Exégèse de Romains et le Mouvement de Keswick*, unpublished doctoral thesis.
14. O. A. Curtis, *The Christian Faith*, p.373.
15. W. H. Griffith-Thomas, *St Paul's Epistle to the Romans*, p.191.
16. Mitton, 'Romans 7 Reconsidered.'

Chapter 2

1. For further study of the structure of the epistle to the Romans see A. Nygren's *Commentary on Romans* published by Fortress Press.
2. J. Murray, *The Epistle to the Romans*, New International Commentary, Marshall, Morgan & Scott, 1967.

3. J. Brown, *Analytical Exposition of the Epistle of Paul the Apostle to the Romans*, Oliphant, Anderson & Ferrier, 1833, p.31.
4. J. Fraser, *A Treatise on Sanctification.*
5. E. F. Kevan, 'The Saving Work of the Holy Spirit,' *The Keswick Week,* 1953, p.32.
6. Murray, *Epistle to the Romans.*

Chapter 3
1. R. Haldane, *Exposition of the Epistle to the Romans,* Banner of Truth, 1963.
2. Fraser, *Treatise on Sanctification.*
3. E. Reisinger, *The Carnal Christian,* Banner of Truth, pp.11-12.
4. W. Hendriksen, *Commentary on Romans,* Banner of Truth.
5. Kevan, *Saving Work of the Holy Spirit,* pp.23-4.
6. Murray, *Romans.*
7. Marcus Rainsford, *Lectures on Romans,* London, 1879.
8. Brown, *Analytical Exposition of Romans.*
9. Fraser, *Treatise on Sanctification.*
10. Calvin, *Commentary on Romans.*
11. Haldane, *Exposition of Romans.*
12. C. Hodge, *A Commentary on Romans,* Banner of Truth.
13. R. C. Lenski, *Romans,* I. C. C.
14. Kevan, *Saving Work of the Holy Spirit,* p.24.
15. Murray, *Romans.*
16. Nygren, *Commentary on Romans.*
17. Murray, *Romans.*
18. H. Ridderbos, *Commentary on Galatians.*
19. Calvin, *Commentary on Romans.*
20. Hodge, *Commentary on Romans.*
21. E. F. Kevan, *Saving Work of the Holy Spirit.*
22. Murray, *Romans.*
23. C. E. B. Cranfield, *A Critical Exegetical Commentary on the Epistle to the Romans,* I. C. C.
24. Lenski, *Romans.*
25. Hodge, *Commentary on Romans.*
26. Cranfield, *Critical Exegetical Commentary on Romans.*
27. In this connection see J. I. Packer's comments in 'The Wretched Man in Romans 7', in *Studia Evangelica II* (41), p.626.
28. Ridderbos, *Commentary on Galatians,* pp.126, 229.
29. Käsemann, *An die Römer,* pp.203-11.
30. Calvin, *Commentary on Romans.*
31. Cranfield, *Critical Exegetical Commentary on Romans.*
32. Packer, 'The Wretched Man in Romans 7', p.626.

33. Cranfield, *Critical Exegetical Commentary on Romans.*
34. As above.
35. Käsemann, *An die Römer,* p.212.

Chapter 5
1. J. Murray, *Sanctification,* p.5.
2. J. Calvin, *Institutes of the Christian Religion,* L 3,VI, 1.4.
3. Murray, *Sanctification,* p.5.
4. B. B. Warfield, *Christian Perfectionism,* p.464.

Appendix I
1. Käsemann, *An die Römer,* p.191.
2. Packer, 'The Wretched Man in Romans 7,' p.625.
3. Nygren, *Commentary on Romans.*
4. J. Denney, *St Paul's Epistle to the Romans,* E.G.T.

Appendix II
1. Warfield, *Christian Perfectionism.*
2. C. Finney, *Views of Sanctification,* 1840, p.168.
3. S. Barnabas, *So Great Salvation,* Keswick Convention, pp.76-82.
4. A. E. Garvie, *Romans,* The Century Bible, p.174.
5. Mitton, 'Romans 7 Reconsidered', pp.184-5.
6. As above, pp.184-5.
7. J. Murray, *Collected Writings,* Banner of Truth, vol.2, p.278.
8. R. B. Gaffin, *Resurrection and Redemption,* p.135. He quotes in support of his statement Acts 20:32; 26:18; 1 Cor. 1:2; 6:11; Eph. 5:25; 1 Thess. 4:7; 2 Tim. 2:21.
9. Murray, *Romans.*
10. A. A. Hodge, *Evangelical Theology,* Banner of Truth, pp.301-11.
11. Murray, *Sanctification,* p.2.
12. Warfield, *Christian Perfectionism.*
13. F. L. Patton, quoted in *Princeton Seminary Bulletin,* 1924.

Appendix III
1. K. Barth, *Christ in Adam: Man and Humanity in Romans 5,* p.30.
2. See C. Van Til, *Christianity and Crisis Theology,* Orthodox Presbyterian Church Committee on Christian Education.

General index

Scripture index